Teaching in the Sciences:
A Handbook for Part-Time &
Adjunct Faculty

Michael Collins

Edition

To order, contact:

The Part-Time Press
P.O. Box 130117
Ann Arbor, MI 48113-0117
734-930-6854
FAX: 734-665-9001

First printing: April, 2011
© 2011 The Part-Time Press Inc.

Library of Congress Data
Catalog Card Number:

ISBN: 978-0-940017-35-1 (paperback)

Printed in the United States of America

Table of Contents

Table of Figures

INTRODUCTION
GETTING STARTED IN THE CLASSROOM

When part-time and contingent lecturers, post-doctoral fellows and graduate students are asked to teach undergraduate science courses at universities and colleges, the courses are often introductory major courses or non-major courses, which often also tend to be large enrolment courses. This book will, therefore, serve not only to provide guidance for teaching majors and non-majors science courses, but also suggestions on how to deal with large classes. This book is based on my many years of teaching experience together with articles written by other teachers and researchers which I have found useful in my own teaching and for student learning.

If you are new to teaching I don't suggest trying all of these ideas straight off but perhaps to try a few to see how they work out for you, and then to try out other ideas as you continue your teaching career. Also bear in mind that what may work for one particular class may not necessarily work for other classes. Different groups of students, even if only different sections of the same class, can react very differently to the same teaching technique, so it is always useful to have a few other approaches up your sleeve.

There are, however, a number of ideas and suggestions that I think everyone should employ and so these are discussed early on in the next chapter.

When I attended university—and I won't say when that was—lecturing was just about the only teaching method that I encountered. Decades later, I suspect, a visit to many science classrooms would reveal that the lecture is still the predominant teaching format, although PowerPoint slides have for the most part replaced overhead projectors and chalk on the chalkboard, as the way to present notes. The widespread use of the lecture as the main way of disseminating information to learners reflects the old idea that learning is a passive process, and that information needs only to be transferred to a learner's brain just as water can be poured into a jug!

"The traditional, behavioristic views of learning that have permeated both psychology and education for at least half a century have thought of learning as being primarily a passive, receptive, and reproductive process. The role of teachers, according to this view, is to dispense information that students can absorb in a more-or-less passive manner and then reproduce at the appropriate time ... One might characterize this approach as "learning from the outside in," and it is still a very influential view if one judges from the teaching practices that can be observed in many many classrooms" (Shuell, 1987).

Over twenty years after Shuell's observation the lecture approach still seems to dominate in university science teaching.

Newer theories of education and psychology emphasize the active nature of the learning process. In a still widely quoted article, Chickering and Gamson, (1987) proposed seven key principles for (undergraduate) education, namely:

1. Encouraging contacts between students and faculty.

2. Developing reciprocity and cooperation among students.

3. Using active learning techniques.

4. Giving prompt feedback.

5. Emphasizing time on task.

6. Communicating high expectations.

7. Respecting diverse talents and ways of learning.

Recent research clearly indicates that students learn more when they are 'actively' involved in the learning process.

"What and how much an individual learns depends on the *activities* in which he or she engages; learning involves more than passively responding to the environment" (Shuell, 1987).

With so many recent advances in educational and psychological research we now know much more about the actual learning process and how information is received, stored, and retrieved (as well as forgotten), and how a multiplicity of factors can affect the learning process. Such factors include, for instance, the nature of knowledge itself (how the subject itself is organized and structured i.e., major concepts and paradigms etc.), the characteristics of students (different personality types and learning styles), different instructional styles (lecturing, cooperative learning, personalized system of instruction, etc.), the prior knowledge of students and their misconceptions about the subject, the stage of cognitive development of the student (concrete versus formal level of operational thought) and so on. In addition there is an every growing body of research that deals with instructional and learning techniques based on recent findings (e.g., concept mapping, advanced organizers etc), as well as a variety of 'newer' instructional and learning strategies (e.g., learning cycle, case studies, supplemental instruction etc.). With the rapid advances in computer-based educational technologies there are numerous articles documenting how such technologies can be used to enhance teaching and learning.

The Problem of Attrition in Science Courses

Another good reason for questioning the way in which students are taught concerns the whole issue of retention of students in the sciences. We know that retention of students in general is a major issue at many institutions, where fewer than half of the students entering as freshmen actually graduate with a degree four or more years later. The situation is even more extreme in the sciences. Dubetz et. al., (2008) point out that historically there has been a high attrition rate in general chemistry courses taught using the traditional lecture/laboratory format. Dougherty et. al., (1995) have cited attrition rates as high as 57 percent in science courses. Another disturbing trend has been the relatively low number of graduates in the fields of chemistry, physics and engineering (National Task Force on Undergraduate Physics, 2002). But why is there such a huge retention/attrition problem in the sciences?

Lord (2008) says that, "Most majors come to college eager to learn and intent on doing well. However, doing well only occurs with a small portion off freshmen wanting to learn science."

He goes on to say that, "Education theorist Sheila Tobias divides science students into two different groups: those who remain with the curriculum and eventually earn a science degree, and those who have the ambition and ability to succeed, but lose motivation and interest in their courses and switch to non-science fields. .... Many students in this second group are discouraged from continuing in science, not because they are incapable of meeting course challenges, but because of the way science courses are *taught* (my emphasis)."

Tobias, (1990) a sociologist by training, who has spent a considerable amount of time studying the teaching of science in colleges and universities says that most all the courses the student takes in science are didactic and teacher-centered, which is not true of the courses taken by non-science majors. She says that there are several pitfalls in the way college science courses are taught that dissuade students from continuing in the major. These pitfalls include:

1. A failure to motivate interest in science by establishing its relevance to students' lives and personal interests;

2. The relegation of students to a passive state in the classroom;

3. An emphasis on competition for grades rather than cooperative learning, and

4. A focus on algorhythmic problem solving as opposed to conceptual understanding.

Researchers such as Gardner (1991) point out that students have different types of learning styles that enable them to learn in different ways and understand at different rates. Tobias (1990) says that while academics in non-science disciplines have adapted their instruction to accommodate the 'learning styles' concept, science professors generally don't alter their way of disseminating information. In fact Bligh (2000) says that the lecture is so ingrained in higher education that over 95 percent of science professors in the nation (U.S.) use it. According to Tobias (1990) this is the major reason for the poor quality of science instruction in our colleges and universities today.

Yet in spite of the fact that research studies conclude that lecturing, by itself, is an ineffectual way of teaching science, it seems that most professors still rely on the lecture as the prime method of teaching, much to the detriment of the students in their classes. You, as instructors of students in introductory science classes can make a significant difference to the teaching of science by adapting your teaching to take account of the different types of students in your classes. Perhaps you can also 'switch on' more students to science majors thereby reducing the atrocious attrition rates in science courses and helping to increase the numbers of students who actually succeed in science and graduate with science degrees!

Before we leave this introductory chapter it would be useful to find out what we should be aspiring to if we intend to be effective teachers. Many studies (e.g. Miller, 1975) have been conducted into what students consider to be the characteristics of good teaching. Even though different studies have come up with slightly different findings most seem to agree that a good teacher is one who:

- is well prepared for class

- has a good knowledge of the subject

- is dynamic and energetic

- is interested in the subject

- has a genuine interest in students

- is fair in evaluation

- encourages student participation

- has effective teaching methods, and

- enjoys teaching.

If then you are genuinely interested in the improvement of instruction, the characteristics of a good teacher listed above, and the teaching tips explained in the rest of this book will put you well on the way to a successful, and enjoyable, teaching career in the sciences!

How To Get the Most Out of This Book.

Keys to Success: Whenever you see this icon, you'll want to take special note because these are tried and true tips to improve your classroom performance.

Caution Light: Whenever you see this icon, you'll know that other successful adjunct and part-time instructors have discovered what NOT to do while teaching.

In addition to the icons, an index has been compiled for ease of use. The table of contents is very detailed to get you to the topic that most interests you at the moment.

So you can read this handbook from front to back or keep it handy as a quick reference on many of the most important areas of concern for new and experienced adjunct and part-time faculty.

This is your quick reference for good teaching. You may use this book as a manual, a guide, or for professional reading. It contains practical and informative tips to assist you with your instructional tasks. It is written in a user-friendly manner for your convenience. Enjoy it and GOOD TEACHING.

CHAPTER 1
TEACHING: WHAT'S IT ALL ABOUT?

Orientation to College and Adult Teaching

In the coming decades, teachers of college and adult students will be faced with many challenges that did not previously exist. Compared to the classroom of former years, the evolution to the modern classroom has caused significant changes. The influx of multicultural and multilingual students, the impact of technology, and the admission of students with differing academic preparation have demanded the attention of educators everywhere. In addition, changing economic and political pressures throughout the world have impacted education and, you, the instructor.

You will feel the impact whether you teach in a continuing education program for business, industry or the military; in a liberal arts college with time-honored traditions and values; in a community college with an open door policy; in a public research university with postgraduate programs; or in an adult education center. The students of today will be more highly motivated, more challenging and in many ways more enjoyable to teach.

With the concern for accountability and the realization that there are established strategies and techniques for instruction, there is greater emphasis upon quality instruction. Adult students employed in business and industry expect a planned and organized classroom. It is no longer a question of whether there are going to be instructional objectives and strategies for teaching; it is a question of how skilled instructors are in developing and delivering them.

One of the most important factors, however, remains the human element of teaching. If you enjoy being a teacher, there is nothing wrong with telling the students that you are there because you enjoy teaching. Being cheerful, open, and understanding is always an asset to good teaching. Students will like to hear your experiential anecdotes — share them. Look upon the class as a project. Adult students expect planning and preparation and will not rebel if it is required. Be aware of your cultural and intellectual environment. Strive to be a good and successful instructor and your teaching experiences will be exciting, rewarding, and satisfying.

It might help you to take a few moments before your first class to meditate about your reasons for teaching. This will do two things: it will encourage you to more clearly identify your personal goals and it will increase your confidence.

There may be students who question why someone with your expertise would spend their time teaching a college course. Be prepared. Have a few answers ready if students ask. If they don't ask, you might want to include it in your personal introduction. You certainly have good reasons. It might be to your advantage to communicate them. You may just enjoy teaching, like interaction with others, like the stimulation, enjoy being in front of a group, or feel it improves your own skills.

You should also give thought to your role in your institution. In short "what is an adjunct/part-time instructor?" Too often adjunct faculty, and thus their students, feel their place within the institution is a temporary and unimportant one. Nothing could be farther from the truth. Adjunct faculty in recent years have assumed a greater responsibility to the educational mission of their colleges and universities. Many institutions depend upon adjunct faculty for 50 percent or more of credit hours of instruction taught. Also in many institutions, adjunct and part-time faculty serve on committees and accept other non-instructional assignments. Finally, adjunct faculty often teach in specialized areas where specific qualifications and expertise is needed. Yes, whether you are a continuing adjunct or a last-minute part-time replacement, yours is an important role and necessary to the integrity and success of your institution.

 As with their full-time colleagues, teaching is still a vocation for many adjunct instructors, a calling to those individuals who enjoy being with people and feel an intrinsic satisfaction in helping others to grow.

In your role as an adjunct/part-time instructor, you will realize many of the intrinsic rewards of the profession. You are repaying your profession for its contributions to your own personal and professional development. There is satisfaction in providing service to your community and you will find that teaching builds self esteem, offers personal rewards, and keeps you intellectually alive. Teaching can provide intellectual growth, community recognition and respect, and the development of new professional contacts. The satisfactions and rewards of being a good adjunct instructor are real and many.

Establishing a Teaching Environment

Over the past two decades, there has been a major movement in higher education called "the learning college" movement or community-centered learning. Quite simply, this means that learning has become student-centered rather than instructor-centered. This is especially important to adjunct faculty members, most of whom come from the surrounding community and thus are aware of community mores.

When establishing a student-centered learning environment, one should first examine the teacher-student relationship. The simple and most obvious way to develop a relationship with your students is be yourself and be honest, establishing communication in the classroom the same as you would in any other human endeavor. There are, however, additional specific steps that can be taken to establish a proper learning environment. Helen Burnstad describes four areas in which the learning environment should be examined: teacher expectations, teaching behavior, physical space, and strategies for creating an environment for learning (Burnstad, 2005). Although it is impossible to describe these areas completely in this handbook, some of Burnstad's major points are examined below:

- Teacher expectations. It is important first, that each instructor have a clear picture of his or her own style and expectations. The expectations that you as an instructor have of yourself may differ considerably from those of the students in your class. This does not mean that you need to change your style. However, you need to examine the expectations of your students in terms of their position (rather than your position) on issues and principles that may arise in class. Also it is important that you consider your own teaching goals. From this you can frame your philosophy and intent regarding the content of the course.

- Teacher behaviors. It is important that you examine your presence in the classroom. Students will sense whether you really love your subject matter or are teaching the course to reach some unrelated professional goal. A pleasant personality is important. Enthusiasm may be demonstrated through energy and engaging in activities with students. Remember, your feelings concerning the expectations of your students will unwittingly be reflected in the success or failure of your students.

- Physical space. Although in most cases you will have little control over the physical aspects of the classroom environment, there are several things that can be done by the instructor. If possible, you may physically move seats so that dialogue and eye contact are easier. You should monitor the attention span of your students; sense the need for reinforcement; calculate the time-on-task; and encourage students to move, interact and ask questions.

- Environmental Strategies. Some strategies that can improve the classroom environment include:

1. **Introducing yourself** to your students with some personal anecdotes.

2. **Being prepared** for students with diverse backgrounds.

3. **Using an activity for getting to know** your students, whether a game, a writing assignment, or reference card, etc.

4. **Learning each student's name** and providing ways for students to get to know one another.

5. **Preparing a complete and lively syllabus.** You can have your students from a previous class leave a legacy by asking them to write a letter for incoming students then sharing it.

6. **Using classroom assessment** techniques.

Finally, whether one is establishing a classroom environment or doing day-to-day activities, it is important that you be as positive in your student-teacher relationships as toward your subject matter. Make yourself available for student contact, either personally or electronically. Take a personal interest in each student and never judge or stereotype students.

Characteristics of Good Teaching

Using one's mind in the pursuit of knowledge and at the same time sharing it with others is very gratifying. The responsibility for a class and the potential influence on students can be very stimulating. It remains stimulating, however, only so long as the instructor continues to grow and remains dynamic.

The qualities of good teaching are quite simple:

- Know your subject content.

- Know and like your students.

- Understand our culture.

- Possess professional teaching skills and strategies.

Knowing your subject means simply that you have a command of your discipline and the capability of calling upon resources. Knowing students is part of the teaching process and is aided by formal and informal communication within and outside the classroom. Understanding our cultural milieu has become increasingly complex for today's instructor. Sensitivity to the diverse cultures in your classroom is necessary to succeed in teaching. Finally, it is necessary that you continue to develop and improve strategies and techniques for the delivery of instruction in the classroom.

Some characteristics that students look for in good teachers are:

- Being knowledgeable, organized, and in control.

- Getting students actively involved in their learning.

- Helping students understand the course objectives and goals.

- Being a facilitator, not a director.

- Knowing the latest trends and technology.

- Stimulating discussion utilizing ice breakers.

- Preparing professional materials and handouts.

The First Class

No matter how long you have been teaching you will always be faced with another "first class." If it is your very first time teaching as an adjunct, the strategies you incorporate are not significantly different from those used on the first class of any future course you may teach. There will always be anxieties and some nervousness before the first class. For experienced faculty who have just completed a course where rapport and communication had been developed, you now face a new class where your students are strangers to you and you are a stranger to them. The anxieties of this returning class are the same as those of the very first class that you will or have ever taught. It is often stated that you never get the second chance to make a first impression and this is certainly true in the world of teaching.

In preparing for the first class, keep in mind that it is nearly impossible to anticipate all situations. The speed at which your first class presentation goes will vary from class to class. Many times student response is significantly greater or less than expected. Having excessive material prepared for the first class will allay this problem and is worth the extra effort in confidence gained.

Another stress reliever when facing your first class is knowing yourself as a teacher. Anyone mature enough to be teaching has some feeling of his or her own personal characteristics. Most of us are average in appearance; however, we usually have gone through life compensating for our variations from the average. There is no more need to be self-conscious in front of a class than there is in any social situation. However, minor compensations may help. If you have a tendency toward casual or even sloppy appearance, appearing neat and professional will pay off. If you have a light voice, practice in expression may be well worth the time spent. Generally speaking, students' first impression of you will include your appearance and actions. If you are timid — take charge. Being in control pays off not only in eliminating barriers to classroom communication, but in developing self-confidence in teaching.

Since the first class is a form of a social introduction, it will influence all successive meetings. You should have a detailed plan for the first class period which will diminish the threats and anxieties of expecting the unexpected. It might be helpful to speak with other teachers who have taught the class in an attempt to anticipate students' questions or concerns. It is a good idea to physically visit the classroom where you will be teaching before the first day. If possible, find out who your students are, their ages, their background, and any previous courses or prerequisites they may have taken.

Listed below are some suggestions that will help alleviate any anxieties and get your class off to a good start:

- **Plan an activity** that allows students to get involved immediately. It may simply be an information-gathering exercise.

- **Initiate casual conversation** with and among the students prior to presenting the specifics of the course.

- **Share anecdotes**. Students are interested in your background and some of your course-related experiences.

- **Introduce the following items** to your students: the name and number of the course, the objectives of the course, the text(s), syllabus, the dates of all exams, and your grading system. Finally, take a roll call to establish that everyone there intends to be in your class.

- **Make certain you are early**, at least 20 minutes before the start of the first class. If possible, greet your students as they come in the door.

- **Identify course standards** including time required for outside work.

- **Use an icebreaker.** If possible, make it a question that is related to your course but without a specific answer.

- **Take care of housekeeping items** such as breaks and restroom locations.

- **Conduct a class with real course content.** It is important that students immediately understand that coming to class is a work situation with specific goals and purposes.

- Some successful instructors begin their first class by **asking students to write a short paragraph** about themselves and their concerns. Often students are willing to discuss their anxieties. This will help in understanding the class.

Setting the Tone

Education professionals and teacher trainers agree that creating positive feelings about the course is an important goal for any instructor. Often instructors assume that students know they intend to be pleasant, cooperative, and helpful. However, this should not be taken for granted. With differing personalities and types of students in the classroom, faculty members must realize that a positive comment or gesture to one student may in fact be negative to another student. Thus, you should make a concerted effort to be friendly. A smile, a pleasant comment, or a laugh with students who are attempting to be funny will pay great dividends.

In setting the tone of the classroom, permissiveness is sometimes a good strategy. We are all familiar with the old classroom where students were essentially "passive" learners. We are also familiar with situations where excessive permissiveness became a distraction to other students. Teachers of adults must realize that flexibility and permissiveness are important to a proper learning environment and that encouraging creativity and unexpected comments is part of the learning and teaching process. The instructor has ultimate authority so excessive distraction can always be controlled. Instructors need not exercise authority for its own sake. Remember, permissiveness and flexibility requires considerable skill to work. Authority comes with the title of instructor.

Teachers as Actors and Actresses

In reality, teachers are on stage; they are actors or actresses whether or not they recognize and admit it. A teacher in front of the classroom carries all of the responsibility for the success of the performance, and this requires all of the talents of anyone on the stage. Due to modern technology, unfortunately, students compare faculty to professionals they have seen in other roles. Thus, adjunct faculty must be alert to the ramifications of poor presentation. Faculty members have within themselves all of the emotions of stage performers but with greater audience interaction. There may occasionally be an emotional reaction in class and you should prepare for it. As an instructor, you will experience fear, joy, and feelings of tentativeness, but also feelings of extreme confidence and satisfaction. Handle fear with good preparation; confidence brought forward with good preparation is the easiest way to lessen fear. Remove anxieties from the classroom by developing communication systems. Some adjunct faculty members are effective at using humor.

As a general rule, however, humor should be used delicately. Jokes are completely out. Almost any joke that is told will offend someone.

Classroom Communication

Many kinds of communication exist in every classroom situation. You must be aware that facial expressions and eye contact with students, as well as student interactions, are all forms of communication. It is your responsibility to ensure that classroom communication is structured in a positive manner. Communication starts the moment you enter the classroom for the first class session. The communication methods you use during the first class and the initial interaction with students are indicative of the types of communication that will exist throughout the course.

The amount of student participation as the course progresses is an indicator of the direction in which the communication is flowing; more is always better. Since many students today are adults, there is greater opportunity to call upon their experiences. The discussion of facts, events, examples, analogies, and anecdotes will often elicit an association for your adult students. This will encourage students to share experiences and anecdotes of their own.

Do not assume that classroom communication can only be between the instructor and students. Communication in the classroom can take any number of forms. It can mean a room full of small group activities where students are discussing and interacting with each other as the instructor stands silently by. It can also include animated and serious discussions and even disagreements while addressing a specific problem or issue presented in class. As the instructor, one of your major responsibilities is to provide a setting where students can communicate freely and provide an instructor-directed vehicle that maintains positive goal-oriented communication.

Some specific instructor-led communication activities include the use of open-ended questions, critical thinking techniques, anecdotes, and problem-solving activities. Communication activities between students include buzz groups, a partner system, student panels, collaborative learning activities, student group reports, brainstorming and group discussions. Remember, a good class is dynamic, participative, and interactive.

The Three Rs of Teaching

Everyone remembers the three Rs of learning. For any instructor, however, the three Rs of teaching, are equally important.

The three Rs of good teaching are: repeat, respond, and reinforce. Very simply, student comments and contributions, if worthy of being recognized in class, are worthy of being repeated. A simple repeat, however, is not sufficient. You should elicit an additional response either from the class or the student making the original statement. After the response, you should offer a reinforcement of the statement or add your own conclusions. These three simple rules improve class relationships by emphasizing the importance of student contributions, relationships between students, and the instructor's respect for all the students. This promotes two-way communication and represents the application of one of the basic tenets of learning—reinforcement.

Teaching Styles

Just as students have styles of learning, faculty have their own styles of teaching. Whether your style is one of planned preparation or a natural development, your style is important. For example, an instructor who emphasizes facts in teaching will have difficulty developing meaningful discussions with students who have progressed to the analysis stage of their learning. It is not important that part-time instructors modify their behavior to match that of students. It is important, however, that part-time faculty recognize their own teaching styles and adapt teaching processes, techniques, and strategies to enhance their most effective style. Some questions to assist you in determining your teaching style are:

- Do I tend to be authoritative, directional, semi-directional, or laissez-faire in my classroom leadership?

- Do I solicit communication with and between students easily or with difficulty?

- Am I well-organized and prepared?

- Am I meticulous in my professional appearance or do I have a tendency to put other priorities first and show up in class as is?

A common mistake for many instructors is that they assume their students will learn in the same manner in which the instructor learned as a student.

Therefore, it would be wise to examine some of the basic learning styles of students, discussed in detail in Chapter Two, page 41. By understanding student learning styles, you can modify your teaching techniques to be certain that your presentation style does not turn off certain students.

For example, if you tended to learn best from a direct no-nonsense instructor, then chances are you will lean toward that type of behavior in your own teaching. This would satisfy students who learn in that manner; however, there will be students in your class who are more successful in a more laissez-faire-type environment that gives more freedom of expression. If you thrive on open communication and discussion in your learning process, expecting this from all of your students may be a false hope since many students are silent learners and may be intimidated by the need to verbally participate in class.

These are only a few examples of the types of teaching style adjustments that may be necessary to become an effective facilitator of learning. I have found that teaching styles are not static. Many of the techniques I used early in my career with younger students who appreciated humor and diversion were not as effective later with more mature students who felt they were there to learn, not to be entertained. I also noticed later in my career that although I was well-organized, had well-stated objectives, used good class communication, and observed the characteristics that I deemed important to good teaching, I had become too serious. For that reason I now occasionally mix in with my lesson plan an additional sheet that says to me, "smile, be friendly, smell the roses."

Also, I have found an evolution in the use of anecdotes. Strangely enough it was the reverse. Early in my career the use of anecdotes sometimes drew criticism from students as "too much story telling," or "more war stories." Later I began to put the question on my evaluation questionnaires: "Were the anecdotes and stories meaningful?" The overwhelming response from adult students was "yes." They were pertinent, they brought meaning to the class, and they were valuable because the adults were interested in real life experiences rather than rote lecturing.

 One note of caution, however, the use of anecdotes should relate to the topic being discussed and not simply stories of other experiences. In general, however, most of today's students will approve of anecdotes and may have their own to contribute.

If you wish to do a quick analysis of your style, it can easily be done using the Internet. One such survey is "Gardner's Multiple Intelligences," available on most major search engines. This survey allows you to examine your strengths in eight categories, allowing you to analyze your own strengths and weaknesses in relation to your students. Although you need to be aware of copyright restrictions, many sites have surveys available with copyright permission granted so you can even use them in class.

A meaningful exercise might be to have your students complete the survey on their own (it is non-threatening) and discuss the composite results and what they mean in class.

Professional Ethics

Although the teaching profession has been slow (compared to other professions) to address ethical issues, developments of the past few decades has encouraged an examination of the ethical status of college faculty. Although the recent attention has been inspired by legal or public relations concerns, there has always existed an unwritten code of ethics for teachers based upon values that have evolved both within the teaching profession and our culture.

Dr. Wilbert McKeachie states, "Ethical standards are intended to guide us in carrying out the responsibilities we have to the different groups with whom we interact" (McKeachie, 2002).

Some institutions have adopted written standards of ethical behavior expected of all college faculty. A compilation of some of these standards is listed below as an example and all adjunct/ part-time faculty should check with their department director or dean for information on their institution's standards. For clarity, the guidelines are presented in two categories: those pertaining to the profession of teaching and those pertaining to students.

Ethics and the Profession. This section is an attempt to emphasize the ethical expectations of the profession and the institution in which part-time faculty are employed.

Adjunct faculty:

- Will attend all assigned classes with adequately prepared materials and content as described in the course description.
- Will not attempt to teach a course for which they are not qualified and knowledgeable.
- Will present all sides on controversial issues.
- Will conduct a fair evaluation of students, applied equally to all.
- Will not promote outside entrepreneurial activities

within the class setting.

- When reasonably possible, will attend college orientations and other development activities presented for the improvement of their role as an instructor.
- Will avoid behavior that may be interpreted as discriminatory based upon gender, age, social status or racial background.
- Will hold their colleagues and institution in highest respect in their actions and communication within and outside the institution.

Professional Ethics and Students. This section relates to ethical considerations concerning students.

Adjunct faculty:

- Will not discuss individual students and their problems outside of the professional structure of the institution.
- Will refer student personal problems to qualified staff.
- Will maintain and honor office hours and appointments with students.
- Will respect students' integrity and avoid social encounters with students which might suggest misuse of power.
- Will not attempt to influence students' philosophy or their positions concerning social and political issues.
- Will not ask students for personal information for research purposes.

These guidelines are quite general; however, they provide a vehicle for examining more closely the expectations of the institution in which you teach. Unfortunately, in today's world, there is sometimes a fine line between ethical issues and legal issues.

More formal statements of professional standards are available in the American Association of University Professors, "Statement on Professional Ethics," adopted in 1987, as well as from the National Education Association. For purposes of brevity, refer to the NEA's "Commitment to the Student" under the Code of Ethics of the Education Profession.

The educator strives to help each student realize his or her potential as a worthy and effective member of society. The educator therefore works to stimulate the spirit of inquiry, the acquisition of knowledge and understanding, and the thoughtful formulation of worthy goals.

In fulfillment of the obligation to the student, the educator—

- Shall not unreasonably restrain the student from independent action in the pursuit of learning.
- Shall not unreasonably deny the student's access to varying points of view.
- Shall not deliberately suppress or distort subject matter relevant to the student's progress.
- Shall make reasonable effort to protect the student from conditions harmful to learning or to health and safety.
- Shall not intentionally expose the student to embarrassment or disparagement.
- Shall not on the basis of race, color, creed, sex, national origin, marital status, political or religious beliefs, family, social or cultural background, or sexual orientation, unfairly:
  a. exclude any student from participation in any program.
  b. deny benefits to any student.
  c. grant any advantage to any student.
- Shall not use professional relationships with students for private advantage.
- Shall not disclose information about students obtained in the course of professional service unless disclosure serves a compelling professional purpose or is required by law.

Academic Dishonesty

Academic dishonesty usually appears in two forms: either outright cheating or plagiarism. The problem of cheating in college classrooms has probably become more common in the last few years due to the pressures on students to succeed. Adding to the problem is the fact that we offer student instruction in conducting research on the World Wide Web, which in turn leads to temptation to copy materials from the Web rather than to conduct research.

To minimize cheating, some instructors place a significant percentage of the student evaluation in the form of shared or active student participation. These activities are evaluated for all members of the group, thus providing no incentive for individuals to attempt to cheat to better themselves. It is important also that in the classroom environment ethical responsibilities requiring trust and honesty are emphasized. Of course, the traditional method of countering cheating is to develop multiple tests with different questions and to not repeat the same test or test questions term after term.

Regardless of the amount of trust built in a classroom situation, all exams should be proctored and you should never leave the room in which an exam is being conducted. The instructor is ethically responsible for this commitment to the students who are striving honestly to achieve their goals and make their grade and to the institution. Obviously, extra time spent by the instructor to devise an evaluation plan in which written tests are only part of the final grade is time well spent. Lastly, on the final exam, students may be asked to write in their own words the two or three principles that affected them most in the course and what they feel they may gain in the future. This question could represent a significant part of the final grade.

If you suspect or encounter a student in the act of cheating or plagiarism, the student should be made aware of the situation. This should be done in confidence in a face-to-face meeting.

In the legalistic world we live in, there can only be one conclusive bit of advice: as an instructor, you must be aware of your institution's official procedures and the legal status of your position.

Suspecting someone of cheating or actually seeing is an unpleasant experience; however, it will likely happen in your teaching experience sooner or later. Usually, reasonable rational procedures will adequately cover the situation without the destruction of the student's academic career or standing.

To learn more about academic dishonesty and how to deal with it, refer to "Promoting Academic Integrity in Higher Education," by Pamela Boehm, Madeline Justice and Sandy Weeks, published in 2009, **<http://www.schoolcraft.edu/pdfs/cce/15.1.45-61.pdf>**

In addition, you may want to visit the Web site of the Center for Academic Integrity at **<http://www.academicintegrity.org>**.

Checklist for Part-Time Faculty

There are many things that you need to know when receiving your teaching assignment. There are, however, basic items that will almost assuredly be asked sometime during class. This section lists information you may wish to check before entering the first class. (After reviewing this list, it is recommended that a personal timeline be developed including these and other important dates related to teaching the course.)

Figure 1.1—Faculty Checklist

1. What are the names of the department chairperson, dean, director and other important officials?

2. Have I completed all of my paperwork for official employment? (It's demoralizing when an expected paycheck doesn't arrive.)

3. Is there a pre-term faculty meeting? Date_____
   Time_____

4. Is there a departmental course syllabus, course outline, or statement of goals and objectives available for the course?

5. Are there prepared departmental handouts?

6. Are there prepared departmental tests?

7. Where is and/or how do I get my copy of the text(s) and support materials for teaching the class?

8. Is there a department and/or college attendance or tardiness policy?

9. When are grades due? When do students receive grades?

10. Is there a college or departmental grading policy?

11. Where can I get instructional aid materials and equipment, films, videotapes, software? What is the lead time for ordering?

12. Is there a student evaluation of instruction form for this course? Do I have or can I get a sample copy?

13. Where can I collect background and demographic information about students and their expectations?

14. Who are some of the other faculty who have taught the course? Are they open to assisting adjuncts?

15. Where can I find information to develop a list of resources and references pertaining to outside student assignments?

16. Have the course objectives been reviewed to be certain they reflect changes in text materials or technology?

17. Do I have a variety of instructional strategies planned so that my course does not become repetitious?

18. Do I have a current academic calendar that lists the length of term, the end of quarter, semester, or inter-term for special assignment so everyone clearly understands the beginning and termination of the course?

NOTES

CHAPTER 2
TEACHING ADULT STUDENTS

Although it is impossible to prepare a standard plan that fits all classes, there are some fundamental principles and activities for teaching adult students. Keeping in mind that even these activities must be constantly reassessed to meet changing institutional and cultural needs, this chapter provides a better understanding of today's students so that an appropriate classroom assessment can be made.

Student Characteristics

Today's students, whether they are older adults or just out of high school, possess some common expectations that effect classroom attitudes. These attitudes are based upon students viewing themselves as consumers of a product, rather than seekers of knowledge. As indicated earlier, they will expect well-planned and prepared course goals and objectives. Other recognizable characteristics include:

- Today's students are more self-directed than their earlier counterparts. In other words, they generally know what they want and where they are going.

- Today's students are highly demanding as consumers. They feel that, since they are paying for their education, they are entitled to a product. There have been legal cases in which colleges have been required to provide evidence of delivering advertised services (classes).

- Today's students often come to the classroom with rich life and educational experiences. They have read broadly and often have had interesting employment and/or travel experiences they may wish to share.

- Today's students expect to be treated as adults. They want to be treated as equals, not as students or "kids."

Although the students are more demanding, they are also more interesting, more challenging, and will contribute to a stimulating learning experience if given the opportunity. Most adult students are not in the classroom to compete. They are there to succeed and improve themselves. As a teacher of adults, you should minimize competition and increase cooperation to foster success. Above all, the age-old process of "x" number of A's, "x" number of B's, etc. based upon a bell curve, has been abandoned in the modern classroom.

The Modern Student

The modern student is sometimes described as "the generation Y student" or an "Echo Boomer." Many say that such a label is no more definitive than trying to describe a teenager. Those that dwell on the "generation Y" concept often describe the group as more racially diverse: One in three is not Caucasian. One in four lives in a single-parent household. Three in four have working mothers. While the boomers who are teaching the courses may still be mastering Microsoft Windows 2000, Echo Boomers have been tapping away at computers since nursery school.

In her research paper, "Teaching Gen-Y: Three Initiatives," Dr. Susan Eisner, an Associate Professor of Management at Ramapo State University writes, "To say Gen Y is technologically literate is an understatement" (Eisner, 2004).

Dr. Bob Lay, Dean for Enrollment Management at Boston College, writes that Generation Y students are curious, bright, and highly motivated scholars. "We're getting freshmen who are so prepared for college they're like transfer students."

Accustomed to the Internet, Generation Y students expect and demand instant service. "It puts pressure on the adults," observes Dean Lay. "We're telling our faculty they better use that laptop and start a Web site, because these freshmen want to hit the ground running."

According to Dr. Eisner's research, Gen Y-ers tend to naturally challenge what is being said, and have a "prove it to me mentality." In order for you as a part-time instructor to challenge these students, it will be necessary to develop teaching strategies and procedures that will draw in these learners. These active activities will include group work, role playing, cooperative learning and other techniques described later in Chapter Nine. On the positive side, be aware that students today, although expecting a certain amount of autonomy, will respond to classroom activities in which they are involved and they see as meaningful. They will probably be interested in topics and work assignments that can be researched on the Internet rather than in print documents and periodicals from the library. To address their needs for immediate gratification, they will expect answers to their questions in class and comments and notes on their tests and quizzes.

In planning your classroom strategies for the modern student, keep in mind that these students want to do something rather than to know something. Class presentation should incorporate a variety of formats including charts, videos, graphics, computer projection and other technological visual aids.

Teaching With the Techniques of Andragogy

If you are the typical part-time instructor today, you were probably first introduced to teaching using the methods of pedagogy. Pedagogy is based upon the teaching of children and is synonymous with the word "leader" (Knowles, 1990). In the past several years, however, the role of the teacher has changed from being a leader or presenter of learning to being a facilitator of learning because the average age of the college student today is closer to 30 than to the 20 years old of a few years ago. This older and more diverse student body will come to class motivated to learn but with a different set of needs. They are likely goal-oriented problem solvers and bring with them a need to know why they are learning something.

Thus came the acceptance of the andragogical model pioneered by Knowles. The andragogical model is based upon:

- **The student's need to know,**
- **The learner's self concept,**
- **The role of the learner's experience,**
- **The readiness to learn,**
- **An orientation to learning, and**
- **Motivation.**

Andragogy has often been called the art and science of teaching adults because it places the student at the center of the learning process and emphasizes collaborative relationships among students and with the instructor—all techniques that work well with adult students. The andragogical model prescribes problem solving activities based upon the students' needs rather than on the goals of the discipline or the instructor.

Developing an andragogical teaching strategy requires a warm and friendly classroom environment to foster open communication. You must be aware that many adults have anxieties about their learning experience and lack confidence. Thus, plan activities that make students feel confident and secure with opportunities for students to share their experiences. It is important that this classroom environment be cultivated and nurtured in the first class session and that you establish yourself as a partner in learning and not an expert who has all the answers.

To incorporate the techniques of andragogy in your class, it is necessary that you become proficient in executing student-centered activities including: conducting a meaningful discussion, stimulating cooperative learning, developing good questions and critical thinking strategies, and involving all students in the learning process.

Student-Centered Learning

Student-centered learning is more than just implementation of adragogical strategies. As an adjunct faculty member, it would be wise for you to review your institution's mission statement or statement of philosophy. Many institutions in recent years have gravitated toward the concept of student- or client-centered learning. Institutionally, this may simply mean that the institution is striving to deliver their educational products to students anyplace at any time. Although the institution may be striving to meet the individual needs of the students, student-centered learning may or may not mean that the philosophy or purpose of the institution will change to adapt to all of the students' needs.

In the classroom, however, student-centered learning takes on a different meaning. Most contemporary institutions have adopted many educational delivery strategies to accommodate students in many ways in order to assist them in meeting their educational needs. In a learner-centered classroom, faculty are expected to implement strategies that allow students more self-determination in how they reach their goals. This objective is, however, tempered by the need of departments and disciplines to set explicit achievement standards that must be met to fulfill the goals of the academic discipline.

Some questions you may need to ask yourself to assess your goal of a student-centered learning environment are listed below.

- Do I have strategies to encourage **open communication** among students and between students and the teacher?
- Do I have appropriate **feedback mechanisms** in place so that the feelings and the needs of the students are communicated in a meaningful and timely manner?

- Do I have **collaborative learning strategies** in my lesson plans so students can work as teams, groups, or partners?
- Are the **needs of the students** being met along with the objectives of the course?
- Do I **recognize students as individuals** with diverse backgrounds and needs as well as classroom participants?
- Do I **vary my teaching strategies** to accommodate a wide range of students?

Remember, a student-centered environment does not diminish the responsibility of the teacher nor give the students the power to determine course activities. Rather a student-centered environment requires skillful knowledge and use of cooperative and student-involved strategies implemented by the teacher.

Student Learning Styles

One can easily find many paradigms for student learning styles in educational literature. Faculty are not expected to master or study in detail all of these styles and then attempt to categorize their students. It is, however, useful for you to understand some of the different learning styles that may appear in your classroom so that you can give consideration to individual differences. One such learning style system is called the "4mat system." This system identifies four types of learners. They are: imaginative learners, analytic learners, common sense learners, and dynamic learners.

- **Imaginative learners** will expect the faculty member to produce authentic curricula, to present knowledge upon which to build, to involve them in group work, and to provide useful feedback. They care about fellow students and the instructor.
- **Analytic learners** are more interested in theory and what the experts think, they need details and data, and are uncomfortable with subjectiveness. They expect

the class to enhance their knowledge and place factual knowledge over creativity.

- **Common sense learners** test theories and look for practical applications; they are problem solvers and are typically skill oriented. They expect to be taught skills and may not be flexible or good in teamwork situations.
- **Dynamic learners** believe in self-discovery. They like change and flexibility, are risk takers, and are at ease with people. They may, however, be pushy and manipulative. They respond to dynamic instructors who are constantly trying new things (McCarthy, 1987).

It is important to understand that all or some of these types of learners may be present in any given class. This makes it necessary for the instructor to possess the ability to use a variety of classroom activities.

I recall an experience while teaching that relates to this topic. Having for years been successful in teaching classes by encouraging open communication and maximizing student involvement, I found myself teaching a class in which an acquaintance was enrolled. This person simply would not respond or take part in discussions. Knowing the student to be social and bright, I was not completely surprised that when all the criteria for grades were considered, the individual easily earned an "A," contrary to my belief that all students must participate to learn! It was only later that I realized that the student process for learning was not flawed, it was just different from the style that I, as the instructor, had perceived necessary for learning.

Closely reviewing the description of the student types will bring out another important factor. That is, just as students have learning styles, teachers have teaching styles. Thus, you should be able to identify your own teaching style from the learning style descriptions. Understanding your teaching style will allow you to modify your behavior to accommodate all learners.

After considering the learning styles above, it is just as important to keep in mind two major factors concerning adult learners. First, they have basically been trained to be cognitive learners so they will first seek to obtain the knowledge and information that they feel is necessary to complete the course work and receive a passing grade. Second, adults learn by doing. They want to take part in learning activities based upon their needs and application. When interacting with individual students in your classroom, you must continually recognize that all learners are not coming from the same set of circumstances.

Diversity in the Classroom

If there is any area of teaching that demands common sense, it is the diversity found in today's classrooms. Classes today are full of students of various age groups, ethnic backgrounds, cultural experiences, and educational abilities. This diversity can contribute to a more interesting classroom when interactive learning allows students to learn about different cultures and differing perspectives first hand through debate and discussion.

For the teacher, however, diversity poses significant challenges. While you must be aware of your students' diverse backgrounds, you must be equally cautious not to overcompensate or appear to give special attention to any one group or individual.

There are some specific teaching strategies that can be implemented and of which you should be aware. When contemplating the course content you should consider the age of the students and their experiences. For example, when older students contribute anecdotes, they usually use their own past experiences. While younger students may prefer topics that effect them immediately. In understanding student attitudes and behaviors, keep in mind that many older students were educated in structured classroom settings and are accustomed to formal lecture and discussion formats, while younger students will probably respond to a more active learning style. Older students also will have the confidence to share their experiences and backgrounds with the class whereas younger students may hesitate.

Above all avoid stereotyping any members of our culture. Salomon (1994) makes specific suggestions concerning diversity in the classroom. Some of his suggestions are:

- Do not address students by nicknames. Use the first and last names on the student roster.
- Do not tell or tolerate racist, sexist, ethnic or age-related jokes.
- Do not imply negatives when addressing other ethnic groups or culturally different societies.
- Become aware of your own prejudices.
- Never allow your own personal values to be the sole basis for judgment.
- Constantly evaluate your cultural perceptions to be sure they are not based upon personal insecurities.

Generally keep in mind that the diverse classroom provides several opportunities. Diversity provides an enriching experience when students share with each other and with the instructor and may assist in reducing cultural barriers. The diverse class provides a forum for understanding the differences that exist between individuals and social classes. Through group interactive strategies, these differences can give students the chance to be full participants in their learning and development process. These group strategies can also provide opportunities for all students to become a part of their classroom community regardless of their background.

Bloom's Taxonomy of Educational Objectives

If there is a single paradigm that has stood the test of time in education it is Benjamin Bloom's Taxonomy of Educational Objectives (Bloom et al., 1956). Published more than half a century ago, this taxonomy describes the learning process as three factors or domains. They are the cognitive domain, affective domain, and psychomotor domain.

Essentially, cognitive learning is learning that emphasizes knowledge and information and incorporates analysis of that knowledge. Affective learning centers on values and value systems, receiving stimuli, ideas and to some degree, organization. Psychomotor learning addresses hand/eye coordination, normally referred to as physical coordination.

The importance of these three domains is not so much the overall consideration of the categories as it is the breakdown provided by Bloom. For example, Bloom's cognitive domain is broken into several categories: knowledge, comprehension, application, analysis, synthesis, and evaluation. The affective domain is broken into receiving, responding, valuing, organizing and characterization of value complex. A psychomotor domain essentially is that which provides for the development of physical skills.

The cognitive domain is usually emphasized in the classroom learning situation. However, when writing course objectives it is often expected that all three domains will be represented. This means that you should have objectives in the cognitive domain written not only at the knowledge level but also the evaluation, analysis, and synthesis levels. In the affective domain, you would have objectives covering responding, valuing and value complex. Many institutions require course objectives and activities in all three of the domains of Bloom's Taxonomy. It should be noted from examination of the descriptions rendered here that these domains effectively cover all areas of the learning process.

Motivation

Students are motivated for many reasons: individual improvement, intellectual curiosity, needed employment competencies, career change or advancement, employment requirement, or the completion of degree or certificate requirements. Although these motivational reasons are broad and varied, faculty must possess the skills to motivate students with a variety of activities including occasional risk-taking.

The following anecdote exemplifies such risk taking. After many years of teaching, I remember being faced with a class that would not respond or participate. Admittedly it was a Friday night class; however, you might expect that in such a class, highly motivated students would be enrolled. They were, however, very tired students and many of them were enrolled merely to pick up additional credits. After teaching the class about three weeks and experiencing very little student response, on the spur of the moment during the third evening, I simply stated, "We must start communicating. I would like each of you at this time to turn to a person near you, introduce yourself and tell them that you are going to help them get through the course, no matter how difficult it is, that you will be there to help them whenever they become confused, and that the two of you (by helping each other) can be successful in this course."

This seemingly simple technique worked wonders. The students became acquainted with someone they hadn't previously known, and in many cases, found someone who really could help them get through the course. For the remainder of the course, when it appeared that the class was experiencing difficulty, I simply needed to say "let's take a few minutes and get together with our partner." When chalkboard work was given, two students would voluntarily go to the board together. Thus a previously unused "risk" activity proved successful—and was my first experience with collaborative learning and the partner system. This is an example of trying a basic technique of motivation. In this case it worked. It may not work every time, but it was not a technique that I had in my repertoire prior to that time. So, when motivating adult students, remember that you must occasionally try techniques not necessarily found in the literature; however, there are proven techniques that should be in the professional portfolio of all teachers, such as Maslow's Hierarchy of Needs.

Maslow's Hierarchy of Needs

It is virtually impossible to incorporate all theories of motivation for your students. It is appropriate, therefore, that we find refuge in a time-honored theory of learning called Maslow's Hierarchy of Needs. Maslow's hierarchy states that the basic needs of human beings fall into five categories:

- **PHYSIOLOGICAL—feeling good physically with appropriate food and shelter.**
- **SAFETY—the feeling of security in one's environment.**
- **LOVE AND BELONGING OR THE SOCIAL NEED—fulfilling the basic family and social role.**
- **ESTEEM—the status and respect of a positive self-image.**
- **SELF-ACTUALIZATION—growth of the individual.**

Physiological, Safety, Love and Belonging. The fact that Maslow's needs are in hierarchy form is a major problem for teachers of adults. For example, attempting to address the needs of esteem and self-actualization in the classroom, when physiological, safety, and love and belonging needs have not been met, is a difficult task. In fact, the lack of fulfillment of the basic needs may interfere with the learning process. This interference may manifest itself in anti-social behavior.

The challenge becomes, how does one in a short period of time, teaching on a part-time basis to mostly part-time students, overcome these barriers? The fact is that one may not overcome all of these barriers. If instructors attempt to take the time to analyze each of the unmet needs of each of their students, they will have little time to work toward the goals and objectives of the course.

There is, however, an important factor to support the instructor. It is that the need to achieve appears to be a basic need in human beings. The need to succeed, an intrinsic motivator that usually overcomes most of the other distractions to learning, is the factor upon which successful teachers capitalize.

There is little that faculty can do to help students to meet the physiological, safety, and love and belonging needs. The need for esteem and self-actualization, which are essentially achievement, are areas in which teaching strategies can be implemented.

Esteem. Esteem is the status and respect with which human beings are regarded by their peers and activities faculty members incorporate that assist students in achieving status and self-respect will support fulfillment of the esteem need. This is accomplished by providing an environment in which students can experience success in their learning endeavors. Many learning theorists claim that success in itself is the solution to motivation and learning.

One of the great fallacies of teaching is often stated by students who have succeeded in classes where other students have dropped out. That observation is: "That prof. was tough, but he/she was really good." This may or may not be true. The fact is that being tough has absolutely no relationship to being good. Too often the reverse of this statement is perpetuated when some faculty emphasize toughness as a substitute for good teaching. There is no evidence to suggest that "tough teachers" are better teachers than those who are "not so tough." It is especially discouraging to marginal students who are working hard but find the chances for success negated by the instructor's desire to be tough.

Teaching Adult Students

Building esteem through success is accomplished in many ways. The following are some classroom instruction suggestions to assist students in achieving success:

- Make certain that students are aware of course requirements. Students should be provided with course objectives in written form that tell them what they are expected to accomplish.

- Inform students precisely what is expected of them. This means not only the work or the skills necessary for them to complete the course content, but also the time commitment.

- Give students nonverbal encouragement whenever possible. There are many ways this can be accomplished. Eye contact with students can very often elicit a positive response. Gestures are important. A smile, a nod of the head, just looking at students with the feeling that you find the classroom a pleasant environment is in itself effective nonverbal encouragement.

- Give positive reinforcement at every opportunity. Simple techniques such as quizzes for which grades are not taken, quizzes designed so most or all students will succeed, as well as short tests as a supplement to grading are effective positive reinforcement strategies. Comments written on hand-in papers, tests, and projects are effective ways to provide positive feedback. Of course, the ideal form of positive reinforcement is provided through individual conferences and informal conversations with students at chance meetings.

- Provide a structured situation in which the students feel comfortable. The laissez-faire classroom is generally a lazy classroom. Most educators agree that a structured setting with students participating in activities is much better than an unstructured approach.

- Provide opportunity for student discussion of outside experiences. Some students in your class, who may not be particularly adept in the course content, may have significant contributions and accomplishments to share. One of the greatest builders of esteem is to allow students to share their success experiences with others.

Self-Actualization. Self-actualization, the highest of Maslow's hierarchy, is the realization of individual growth. Such growth is realized through achievement and success. Course planning for enhancement of student self-actualization is the ultimate in successful teaching. The suggestions listed here can assist in the student growth process.

- Each class should offer a challenge to each student. Challenges are presented in a variety of ways. If they are insurmountable challenges they become barriers; therefore, it is important that faculty plan activities appropriate for the course. Grades are challenges. However, grades must be achievable or they cause frustration. Achieving class credit is a challenge. Most students, even though they may not achieve the grade desired, will feel satisfied if they obtain the credit for which they are working. Assigning incompletes and allowing additional time for projects are techniques that will assist students in obtaining credit for their work. Questions, if properly phrased, can become challenges.

- Problem solving. The ultimate challenge in the classroom is problem solving. Problem-solving techniques vary greatly depending upon the subject matter. Although it is impossible to discuss in detail the ramifications of problem solving, this challenge does not lend itself solely to scientific and mathematics classes.

It can also be utilized in many other courses through discussion, professional journals and literature reports, outside projects, case studies, and group work.

- Treat students as individuals. Individual conferences and development of a system to promote interaction between students, their instructor, and other students are important. Many experienced faculty members do not hesitate to share with students their home or business phone number and/or e-mail address and are usually quite surprised at how seldom any are used.

- Be cautious not to prejudge students. Unfortunately, stereotyping still exists today. Faculty must make every effort not to "type" classes or students as "good" or "bad." Such stereotyping will affect grading and attitudes toward the students. Also, there is a good chance that the judgment may be incorrect. There is no place for stereotypes in education.

- Treat students as adults. Many of today's students hold powerful positions in business and industry. It is difficult for them to regard the teacher as someone superior. To adult students, the instructor is just someone in a different role. Above all, don't refer to them as "kids."

- Give consideration to student's personal problems when possible. Giving adult students personal consideration implies that rules concerning attendance, paper deadlines, tardiness, etc., may be flexible when faced with the realities of the lives of adult students. Practice flexibility whenever possible.

CHAPTER 3
PREPARING FOR THE FIRST CLASS

Planning Your Teaching — In a Hurry!

Ideally, the planning for teaching a course should start well before the first class of the semester but for many of you this will not be possible since you will receive your teaching assignments a day or two before the start of the semester, or maybe after the start of the semester when the designated instructor fails to arrive for their assignment! So what can you do when you are given a last minute teaching assignment? Hopefully the department has a course syllabus for you from previous semesters, the textbook has already been selected and is available to students in the institution's bookstore; if not, you really are behind the eight ball! Under such circumstances how on earth are you going to give a good first class when everything seems stacked against you? After all first impressions are the ones that count.

First of all you will need to have a course syllabus, or an outline, ready to give to your students in that first class. At a minimum it should include the course number and title, the name of the textbook, (and hopefully the chapters to be covered), information about the laboratory sessions (if a laboratory course), including the room number, laboratory manual, and when the laboratory sessions start, the assessment methods for the course (tests, examinations, assignments etc.), and finally information about yourself (name, office number, telephone number(s), e-mail address, office hours etc. If you don't have enough time to produce printed copies for each student at least write the information on the board, or on a PowerPoint slide, or the equivalent.

Once this routine administrative-type information has been covered, you may then want to introduce yourself to the class –

where you are from, where and what you yourself studied at college/university, and maybe even your research topics for master's and/or doctoral degrees. If you feel comfortable enough doing so, talk about your work experience, your reasons for teaching, and anything else that you think might be of interest to the students and which gives them some insight about you as a teacher and a person.

Depending on the size of the class you may wish to employ an icebreaker activity for students to get to know each other. As an example, students could get into pairs (or threes or fours) and each could introduce themselves, their background, interests, intended degree program, and the reason why they are taking this particular course. At the end of the exercise, each student is then asked to "introduce" their partner to the rest of the class. Obviously this only works with small classes! In larger classes you might just wish to ask students to introduce themselves to their neighbors on both sides.

Another possible short exercise is to ask each student, anonymously or otherwise, to write down on a piece of paper, file card, or the like, something about themselves, such as the degree they are hoping to complete, their previous background in the subject (none, high school etc.), the reason they are doing that particular course, the other subject(s) they are taking that semester, and any other interests they would like to add (sports, hobbies, other interests, possible careers etc.). These should be anonymous for you to read later on to get an idea of the class, which can help in the way you teach that particular class.

I always think that it is a good idea to do some teaching in the first class meeting so that students learn something about the subject you will be teaching them and to find out about the way you teach and conduct classes – do the student feel that they are going to be comfortable with your teaching style, and that you are knowledgeable about your subject? Even a short 10 or 15 minutes teaching segment is better than ending that first class early and not having done any teaching. It reminds me of a neighbor who was enrolled at university the first time and when classes actually started was keen to learn about a new subject he had opted to take. He was looking forward to finding something about this new subject but the instructor spent the whole of the first class talking about the administrative aspects of the course but never talked about the subject or gave a lecture. My neighbor came out of that class really disappointed that he had not learned anything about the subject he was so looking forward to studying. It is worthwhile remembering that while there will be students whose only interest is getting out of the classroom as quickly as possible there are those there who actually come excited to learn.

Another option, if you haven't had a chance to prepare even a short lecture, is to ask the students about their prior knowledge of the material you will be covering in the second class. If, for instance, you were to be teaching about cells and cell organelles in the second class you could put a diagram on the board, overhead projector etc., or even take a model of a cell to class and ask students the name of each organelle, and its function. This would serve as an opportunity for students to recall information from a previous course and, if nothing else, helps students to get back into a study mode after their vacations, and to recall information they should have learned in previous classes or in high school. If students are not prepared to answer your questions publicly, you could even try this exercise as an individual or, even better, as a group test. At the end of the test you can ask how many scored at least 50 percent, 75 percent and even 100 percent. At least this way you will know how much background or pre-requisite information you will need to provide in the second class.

The Ideal Way of Planning a Course

Hopefully you will have more than an hour's or a day's warning of the course you are going to teach. If this is indeed the case you will have a little more time to prepare yourself for that first class. Teaching doesn't start with your first class of the semester since a good teacher plans well in advance of the start of any semester.

Preparing for the First Class

Among these preparations should be the following:

- Course outline preparation
- Text book choice
- Writing behavioral objectives
- Laboratory manual (if a lab course)
- Evaluation methods
- Assignments
- Developing course web site
- Lecture preparations
- Statement about plagiarism
- Office hours
- Placing books on reserve in library
- Developing pre-tests (if required)
- Preparing procedures on test re-marking etc.
- Developing the assignment attachment

Clearly then there is a fair amount of work to do well before you actually teach your first class. If you are teaching part-time, and especially in large multi-section courses a number of the items listed above, will have been done for you. In all probability the textbook for the course has already been selected but you will need to read it since this will be your students' main source of information outside of formal classes and so you should be familiar with it. Nowadays most science textbooks come with a whole variety of accompanying materials including audiovisual material, CD's or DVD's, web site information, and on-line self tests, as well as test data banks that you can use to generate test items, mostly multiple choice. Others may also come with student guides and electronic clickers (See "Student Response Systems," page 71.). You may also be provided with a course outline, including the evaluation methods, and in multi-section courses the tests may be prepared by more senior faculty with your own responsibility being to just mark the exams. In large classes you may be assigned one or more teaching assistants to assist you with marking. Evaluation, assignments and teaching large classes are all dealt with in subsequent chapters. If a course outline is provided you will need to add in your own personal information (name, title, office number, telephone, e-mail etc.) before it is ready to be distributed to students.

The Course Syllabus

When Erikson and Strommer (1991) asked students at the end of their freshman year about what instructors might have done to help them, one of the three most frequent responses was to "provide a better syllabus." These authors say that a good syllabus will let students know "where the course will take them, how they are going to get there, and who is responsible for what along the way." Lewis (1994) says that a good syllabus will probably be more than two pages long and will contain the following:

Names, number and required texts, (i.e., course title and number, classroom and time slot, instructor's name, office, phone number, office hours etc., text titles and how they are to be used etc.) It will also include:

- Introduction to the subject matter and course goals

- Description of evaluation procedures

- Overview of class activities and assignments

- Course outline (including week-by-week schedule of topics, readings, assignments; exact dates of exams, assignment deadlines etc.)

- Course policies (including policies for attendance, make-up work, late assignments; statements about student conduct in large classes.)

Lewis's suggestions for the syllabus seem to me to be excellent and should serve as a good guide for a syllabus. Since Lewis's suggestions were published before the general acceptance and use of e-mail and other computer-based technologies I would also add to her list the e-mail address of the instructor, class web site, blog address (if used), and other social network technologies used with the course. I would also add a plagiarism policy to the list of course policies.

Course Objectives

In previous years it was more common to provide behavioral or performance objectives to students giving a list of the desired outcomes they were expected to exhibit by the end of the course. Even though it takes time to write up good behavioral objectives, they are useful in a variety of ways. Not only do the students know exactly what is expected of them, but it is then easier to construct tests and exams, since the questions are phrased to see if students have achieved these objectives. Behavioral objectives are also useful in deciding how and what to teach as the course material should cover these objectives. Sometimes you may find that the objectives, as written, are impossible to teach, and students to learn, and/or to test, in which case it may be necessary to revise the objectives. You can also start each class by telling students which objectives you are dealing with that day.

E-mail, Web Sites, etc.

Nowadays with the popularity of on-line computer tools such as Desire2Learn (D2L) a lot of the material that formerly had to be typed, photocopied and distributed to students can be placed on a class web site, together with on-line notes, links to web sites, text references, and even example tests. Such programs can also be used as forums for students to discuss topics from class, ethical questions arising from material and the like. It saves a lot of time if, in advance, you tell students when to use e-mail to send you a message (items relating to personal matters) and when to use web discussion (asking general questions which other students, in addition to yourself, may be able to answer; discussion topics; and as a means of you making announcements to the whole class about test times etc). Discourage students from asking content-based questions by e-mail as answers posted on a class web site are there for all students to read, and not just the student asking the question. Conversely, messages of a personal nature should not be posted on the class web site.

Office Hours

Many institutions require that each instructor have a minimum number of office hours and these should be posted for students to see. You may find, however, that a large number of your students may not be able to utilize those office hours because of timetable scheduling difficulties and so you may need to adjust some of your office hours. Nowadays with e-mail many students will contact you through that medium rather than visit you in person.

Policies

You may also find it useful to prepare in advance some time-saving procedures, particularly for remarking tests.

 There will always be a number of students who are dissatisfied with their test scores and in large classes this could become a real concern.

Develop a hand-out which explains your procedure for remarking tests. A copy of my sheet is shown in the chapter on evaluation, Figure 11.1, page 130. You can adapt it to your own needs.

Another test-related issue is that of students missing tests for a variety of reasons (medical, attending other "official" events, taking part in sporting events etc.) so develop a policy statement explaining your procedures for dealing with these absences, as well. In the chapter on evaluation I deal with this issue in more detail.

Preparing for the First Class

It is essential to have a policy related to plagiarism. While many institutions have official statements on what plagiarism includes, and how instances of plagiarism are dealt with, it is useful to explain plagiarism to students and how it is dealt with in your institution. If the institution does not have a policy yet, it would be important to have a policy or statement prepared in advance. There are a number of different software companies marketing plagiarism-detecting programs (i.e. Turnitin.com) and some colleges and universities use such software programs to check student assignments.

So far we have just dealt with preparing mostly administrative aspects of teaching a course, but what about preparing the actual classes? Ideally it would be nice to have all your classes prepared ahead of the semester but let's face it—most of us don't have that luxury. Besides, you may find that you need to adjust your teaching to the specific requirements of a class. If you have the first two to three weeks of classes prepared before the start of the new semester, you're doing very well.

Preparing for each class should include:

- Material to be covered

- Objectives to be covered

- Concept map of material

- Activities to be employed

- Learning styles included

- Audio Visual aids

- Summary

- Class notices

It is also useful to take the time to evaluate each section of a course you teach. Note any changes you would like to make the next time you teach that course. Good ideas will be lost from your memory if you don't write them down.

The First Class

First Class Checklist, Figure 3.1

Prepare course outline (see Figure 1.1, page 34.)

Select text book(s)

Write behavioral objectives

Prepare laboratory manual (if a laboratory course)

Develop evaluation procedures

Develop assignments

Construct tests

Develop course web site

Prepare statement on academic honesty

Decide on office hours

Place books on reserve in library (if needed)

Develop pre-tests (if required)

Write procedures on missing tests, re-marking tests, etc.

Develop assignment hand-out

No matter how much preparation you do well ahead of your first actual class, it is still a case of "first impressions count most." So what should you do to make sure that the first class goes well?

There are instructors who use the first class to introduce the course and themselves to the class and then finish. They don't do any teaching until the second class. Start the way you intend to continue— that is to teach.

Preparing for the First Class

It is important to arrive early in the classroom, and to come fully prepared. If possible, visit the actual classroom before and figure out how to correctly use the audiovisual equipment. Make sure you know how to turn on/off the room lights, and have a working microphone if it is a large room which requires the use of an amplifier. If you intend to distribute materials to the class, have them available at the door, or distribute them during the class time.

 Stand by the door of the classroom on the first day. Personally welcome each student as they arrive and hand out any printed materials that are to be distributed. Obviously, this type of welcome is easier to do with a small class, but it's worth the effort as it gives the impression that you're interested in having the students there.

At the start of a new class, I briefly introduce myself and the course, and make reference to the evaluation scheme. I then tell the students that I will be teaching this period. I give an overview of what I intend to cover (behavioral objectives, concept map etc.), and then start to teach. I teach for approximately 12-14 minutes, and then take a two-minute break (having explained its real purpose). After that, I give another mini-lecture.

I finish the class with a student activity as a way of allowing them to get to know their classmates, and to indicate that my classes involve students in their own learning.

When talking about the "Scientific Method," I use an activity which describes a particular experiment and then asks students to form small groups to work out the good and poor features of the experiment and how the experiment could be improved. I give students about ten minutes for the activity, and then ask groups to give me first, the good aspects, and then the poor aspects, and write the responses on the board. Then, I ask for ideas as to how to improve the experiment, and again note these points on the board. The class ends with a summary of what we have covered during this first class.

A first class such as this sets the scene nicely for the rest of the semester. The students will have seen how well-prepared and efficient you were, understand your teaching style, and that you involved them in a student-centered activity. A good teacher is recognized as one who is well prepared, has a good knowledge of the subject, and shows a passion for teaching and their subject and so it is important to convey these characteristics in the first class. Show your enthusiasm for teaching, your subject, and your interest in students.

Figure 3.2—Sample Course Outline

Achievement University
Basic Statistics 101 Course Outline

I. Introduction
    A. Basic statistics—use and purposes
    B. Data gathering
        1. Instruments
        2. Recorded data
        3. Machine utilization
II. Presenting Data
    A. Tables
        1. Summary tables
            a. Table elements
            b. Tables with averages
    B. Graphs
        1. Types of graphs
            a. Bar
            b. Pie chart
            c. Line graph
        2. Data presentation with graphs
    C. Frequency distributions
        1. Discrete and continuous
        2. Class intervals
III. Descriptions and Comparison of Distributions
    A. Percentiles
        1. Computation of percentile
        2. Inter-percentile range
        3. Percentile score

B. Mean and standard deviations
    1. Computation of mean
        a. From grouped data
        b. From arbitrary origin
    2. Variance formulas

C. Frequency distributions
    1. Measures of central tendency
    2. Symmetry and skews
    3. Bimodal distributions

IV. Predictive or Estimate Techniques
A. Regression
    1. Graphic application
    2. Assumption of linearity
B. Correlation
    1. Computation of correlation coefficient
    2. Reliability of measurement
C. Circumstances affecting regression and analysis
    1. Errors of measurement
    2. Effect of range
    3. Interpretation of size

V. The Normal Curve and Statistical Inference
A. The normal distribution
    1. Mean
    2. Standard deviation
    3. Characteristics
B. Statistical inference
    1. Employing samples
        a. Randomness
        b. Parameters
    2. Normal Distribution
        a. Standard errors
        b. Unbiased estimate
        c. Confidence interval
C. Testing hypothesis
    1. Definition of statistical hypothesis
    2. Test of hypothesis
        a. Level of significance
        b. One-sided test
    3. Computing power of test

CHAPTER 4
TECHNOLOGY IN THE CLASSROOM

Oh boy – how technology in the classroom has changed, and how dramatically! When I started teaching, the main piece of technology I used was the overhead projector, occasionally a 35 mm slide projector, and perhaps a 16 mm film projector. Since that time, technologies have come and gone. Technology has always been changing, and the good instructor should be prepared to incorporate new technologies which may assist in the instructional and learning process.

Clearly, the single biggest innovation in educational technology has been the introduction of the personal computer. Early computer pioneers such as Bork (1981) held out great promise for the use of computers in education arguing that computers could improve student learning, "Fundamentally the major factor in interaction. The fact that the computer can make learning an active as opposed to a passive process. . . ."

The computer, according to Bork (1981) would allow us to move away from "spectator" learning and move instead to "interactive" learning for all our students. Computerized testing, computer-assisted learning, and computer-managed learning all had some impact on education, as did computer simulations, but it was only with the advent of the Internet and e-mail that computers really started to have a dramatic effect on education.

No longer are instructors and students limited to information gleaned from books and journals, for the World Wide Web places the whole world at one's disposal. Communications are almost instantaneous, and mobile communication devices allow us to access information and communicate with others wherever we are. Information is no longer restricted to the lecture room and the library, and as instructors we have to realize that the whole instructor-student dynamic has changed. So how best to decide on the place of technology in the teaching and learning process?

Earlier internet-based communication methods such as e-mail, and web sites, are now referred to as Web 1.0. The newer internet-based technologies are now referred to as Web 2.0.

For convenience sake I have arranged the rest of this chapter according to presentation technology/software, communications, learning management systems, Second Life and response systems although strictly speaking the applications we will discuss are not easy to pigeon hole into just one of each of these categories.

Presentation Technology/Software

By presentation I refer to equipment/programs that we can use to present information in the classroom. Many science instructors use the computer and computer projector to "present" their notes in class, usually using presentation software such as PowerPoint. As such presentation software has evolved, it has been used not just to present notes (words) but also visuals (photographs, tables, graphs) and dynamic materials (simulations, audio, video, etc.), and can also be linked to the Internet to access remote sites.

 Many instructors spend a tremendous amount of time glitzing-up their presentations with different colors and fonts for text, exciting slide transitions and the like. However, this is not the best use of our time as instructors and students don't learn any better as a result.

Eves and Davis (2007) point out that, "When used incorrectly, or to excess, we find that computer-generated presentations severely limit our ability to engage students."

Tufte (2006) suggests that presentation software is presenter-oriented, not content or audience oriented, and creates a preoccupation with format at the expense of content. He also points out that space limitations on presentation slides lead to over-generalizations, imprecise statements, insubstantial evidence, and weakly argued claims. (As reported in Eves and Davis, 2007).

Eves and Davis (2007) point out that there are many different forms of visual aids and one should use the one most appropriate to the situation. They also write that, "Good presentations stimulate the learner by offering text or imagery to support key points. It is best to keep the number of slides to a minimum." Eves and Davies (2007) also make a very important point when they write that, "Presentation software works best for materials presented visually not verbally."

Many instructors post their presentation software notes on the Internet for their students to access outside of the classroom. This practice leads many students to skip class and use the on-line presentation notes in place of lecture notes.

 Research indicates that students learn better if they construct their own notes rather than being given them. Use presentation software to give only headings or skeleton notes, and to remember Eves and Davis's caution that such software works best for visual materials.

A common fault among presentation software users is to convert all their notes and visuals into that format. Most teaching rooms equipped with computer projection equipment also have a visual presenter, basically an electronic camera mounted over a stage. The presenter camera can be zoomed in (for a larger close-up) or zoomed out (for a more panoramic view). It can be used for projecting images of solid materials (books, models, etc.).

I incorporate multiple visuals to my lectures, such as books, magazine articles, photographs, cartoons, and small animal specimens to make my lectures more visual.

Another use of the presenter is that of a back-up in the case of computer failure. Always bring a printed copy of your PowerPoint slides to class so that in the case of the computer not working or the software freezing. That way, you can use the visual presenter to project the printed (PowerPoint) notes. Most multimedia classrooms also allow instructors to plug in their own laptops to the computer projector. Check the system in advance to see how you can direct output from your laptop to the projector.

Whiteboards

A whiteboard is basically an electronic chalkboard. Software programs can be displayed on the board, as can PowerPoint presentations, and even interactive web sites. The board also allows the user to write other notes or diagrams onto the display and can have them saved for future use. If, for example, you were projecting a PowerPoint presentation and wrote in new information on a slide while it was being displayed, this would allow you to save the old slide with the new material written on it for the next time you use that particular slide.

The newer whiteboards allow you to access web sites and to scroll through images by flipping, just as you would on an iPhone. You can now purchase whiteboards which are overlays on a wall-mounted plasma screen (rather than using a computer projection unit and a screen) and so you can manipulate the whiteboard directly on the touch-sensitive screen. These newer plasma screens are ideal for use in smaller teaching rooms, and are less expensive.

Communications

There are, of course, a number of different methods of communication based on the computer, of which e-mail is the one with which everyone is familiar. However, e-mail is not the best medium for communications between instructors and whole classes of students. E-mail should be reserved for messages of a personal nature between an instructor and the student. Messages from an instructor to a whole class or between class members are better done through a class listserv or web forum. Questions about the course content may be posted on the web forum, and the instructor (or other student) response is posted for all to see. Class notices, such as times and places of exams etc., may also be posted in this way. A web forum may also be used for class discussions on topics of interest. There are a number of other computer-based modes of communication including weblogs (blogs) and Twitter.

Blogs

"A blog is a frequently updated web site consisting of dated entries called posts (including text, images, media objects, and data) arranged in reverse chronological order so the most recent entry appears first" (Brownstein and Klein, 2006).

Brownstein and Klein point out that blogs may be used as virtual environments, where all students may participate in critical discourse on scientific topics. In many ways blogs are similar to web forum postings. Since blogs are well-accepted methods for communicating one's thoughts or ideas, or responding to other people's postings, they are now being used by many college and university professors, although because of their fairly recent appearance on the scene there is little research published on their uses and their effect on student learning.

Brownstein and Klein (2006) write that, "Blogging gives voice to students who often feel uncomfortable speaking up in class and can have a powerful impact on a greater number of students in the classroom as it supports more learning styles." They have identified a noticeable change in the quality and quantity of learning taking place in the classroom since introducing blogs. In particular, the focus has moved from "what" to "why."

Blogs then offer another format for communications in a classroom, and given their current popularity in the Internet world will continue to be electronic communication tools of use in science teaching. (For more information on the use of blogs in science teaching see Brownstein and Klein, 2006).

Twitter

The web site Twitter.com is a more recent communication tool, similar to blogs, but one which limits posts (called "tweets") to just 140 characters. This new tool, like blogs, has potential in teaching and learning, although the limited length of responses does not allow for detailed discussions. However, a recent study at the University of Leicester in the UK discovered that tweeting helped:

develop peer support among students,

develop personal learning networks, and

students to arrange social meetings.

The researchers also found that Twitter was very attractive as a data collection tool for assessing and recording the student experience, with a wide range of free and increasingly sophisticated on-line analysis tools (Cann et al., 2009).

Social Networking Sites

Sites such as YouTube, Facebook and MySpace are very popular social networking sites for students to keep in touch with friends and family. While these sites have a potential for use in education settings, it is not clear that they have immediate applications to teaching. However a number of instructors do use video clips which are posted on YouTube in their lectures, and it's possible to maintain pages on Facebook and MySpace for use by students in their classes to communicate with other classmates and the instructor.

Learning Management Systems

There are a number of different companies marketing learning management software, including Desire2Learn and Blackboard. Usually, the individual college or university has a license for all of the campus so the instructor may not have a choice as to which system to use. My institution, for instance, has decided to use Desire2Learn and offers training for instructors interested in using it. These systems have a number of different components including:

- posting class notes/videos

- links to external web sites

- class web forum

- e-mail to instructor

- posting class notices

- example tests

- class marks register

- links to other educational software packages such as Second Life, blogs etc.

Learning management systems offer the ability to post lecture notes, PowerPoint slides, videos, class announcements, have students submit assignments electronically, to maintain class marks (which individual students can access to find out their own test scores, etc.), and to post on-line tests. Training is required to use such systems.

Second Life

"Second Life is a free on-line multi-user virtual environment (MUVE) that allows users to meet in virtual space, build and manipulate virtual objects, and converse via text or voice over internet protocol (VoIP)" (Atkinson, Wilson and Kidd, 2008).

Second Life allows for the creation of virtual classes where each user assumes a virtual, identity, an avatar, which can be controlled by the user. Since students in a class can have their own avatars, the student remains anonymous. This allows students who are quiet in a live, on-campus class, to use their avatar to ask questions, make statements, and join in discussions which they might not do in on-campus classes. Second Life may be used as an adjunct to a lecture class or as a distance education course. The software may also be used to create three-dimensional simulations, models, demonstrations which students can manipulate, interact with, or store for later use (Atkinson, Wilson and Kidd, 2008). "Different campuses host different types of events, such as scheduled lectures, media screenings, theatrical productions, labs and virtual office hours. Practically anything possible in real life is possible in SL" (Atkinson, Wilson and Kidd, 2008).

This particular application, then, offers an interesting alternative to live classes in the field of simulations whereby students, and instructors, can assume virtual, anonymous, personalities. At the present time, hundreds of North American colleges and universities use Second Life.

Student Response Systems

One problem associated with large classes particularly, is gauging student understanding of the material presented. While some students will ask questions about material they do not understand, it is usually only when marking tests and examinations that the instructor can see whether students really have understood the material presented in class. The recent advent of electronic clickers now presents an opportunity for instructors to check during class on whether or not students understand the material being presented. Clickers present us with a new, instantaneous feedback system. Herreid (2006) writes that, "They provide instant feedback to students and faculty regardless of the size of the class, and have a clear value in socialization, making impersonal classes more intimate. The technology also seems to resonate with students fascination with interactive media."

Clickers are like television remote controls, with numbered buttons that students can push to give an answer, usually to a multiple choice question. Each student's response is transmitted to a receiver which picks them up and feeds the response into a computer. The class results can be viewed by the instructor on the computer screen. The instructor can quickly gauge the level of understanding of the students and can re-teach the material if the clicker responses indicate a less than ideal understanding of the material. Herreid (2006) points out that, "Research on various forms of instructional feedback, all of which can be provided by clicker systems, has indicated direct relationships between feedback and improved student learning (Guthrie and Carlin, 2004)."

Duncan (2005) lists eleven ways in which instructors can use clickers:

- to measure what students know prior to instruction;

- to measure student attitudes;

- to find out if students have done the reading;

- to get students to confront misconceptions;

- to transform demonstrations;

- to increase students' retention of the material they have been taught;

- to test students' understanding;

- to make some kinds of assessment easier;

- to facilitate testing of conceptual material;

- to facilitate discussion and peer instruction; and

- to increase class attendance.

Science textbooks often come bundled with electronic clickers so textbook choice may determine which type is used.

Even though there are only a few published assessments of clicker use, because of their novelty, Herreid (2006) writes that,

- student enthusiasm for clickers is high;

- student attendance is strikingly improved, changing from below 50 percent in the lecture method to over 80 percent when clickers are used;

- student learning appears to be improved;

- faculty enthusiasm is high; and

- student apathy is much less evident.

While there are some disadvantages of clickers (cost, steep learning curve for faculty etc.) Herreid (2006) concludes that these are minor when compared to their advantages. I would certainly advocate using them in teaching undergraduate science.

Technology in the Classroom

If you don't have access to electronic clickers don't despair. You can get most of the advantages of them using non-electronic response systems. I have seen paper/cardboard cubes with different letters and/or colors on each side used to the same effect. When the instructor poses a question, students show (to the instructor) the side of the cube which displays their chosen response. If colored cube sides are used the instructor can quickly estimate how many members of the class have answered the question correctly, and then decide whether to move on to new material or to go over the previous material again.

CHAPTER 5
TEACHING LARGE CLASSES

It is almost inevitable that teaching undergraduate science, particularly at the introductory levels, also means teaching large classes on most college and university campuses. There is a significant difference between the way in which, say, a large class of 300 is taught as compared with a class of 30 or 50.

Over the years I have seen class sizes increase to the point at which 200 is the normal class size for many first and second year classes. Teaching a large class is not just a matter of teaching more students at the same time, for the larger class is taught in a larger room with fixed seating, and the extra numbers of students makes seemingly simple things such as handing back test papers and assignments much more time-consuming. In addition to these problems, one can add a further dimension, that of students feeling anonymous, and being less likely to contribute to class discussions.

In their study of large classes Wulff et al. (1987) noted that students commented on the impersonal nature of such classes which led to decreased motivation. A third factor, according to Wulff et al. (1987) was an increase in noise and distractions ("Rude people who come late, leave early, or sit and talk to their buddies."). Cooper and Robinson (2000) write, "It is a sad commentary on our universities that the least engaging class sizes and the least involving pedagogy is foisted upon the students at the most pivotal time of their undergraduate careers: when they are beginning college."

Large class size, then, brings at least three sets of problems with which to deal, namely a more challenging teaching environment, more time-consuming administrative tasks, and a large anonymous, less involved audience. This chapter will give you some ideas as to how to tackle these challenges, and some practical examples of how to teach large undergraduate science classes.

Syllabus

Lewis (1994) writes that the syllabus becomes a very important document in teaching large classes.

When Erikson and Strommer (1991) asked students at the end of their freshman year about what instructors might have done to help them, one of the three most frequent responses was to "provide a better syllabus."

The Lecture Hall

A large lecture hall is quite different from the average small classroom. This is why you should visit the designated lecture room ahead of the first class to get acquainted with the room. In most such venues, one's voice needs assistance to be projected to the back of the room, and so most lecture theatres are fitted with microphones, amplifiers, and speakers. In all probability, portable microphones will not be left in the room between classes (they have a tendency to "disappear") and will have to be collected from another location prior to the class. If you are using a portable microphone, remember to check the "low battery" warning light — it's important that your microphone not die on you mid-lecture.

Lewis (1994) suggests that you write something on the chalkboard, and then go to the back of the class to see if you can read it from there. Get used to writing large – 3 inches (8 centimeters) is about the *smallest* you can get away with in a lecture theatre situation. Similarly, if you use an overhead projector (still a useful piece of equipment even though it is an "older" technology), or even PowerPoint slides, try to use a font and size which can be read easily, even in the back row.

Next, find out where the light switches and dimmers are. Check to find out where other relevant controls are positioned (speaker volume control, electronically operated screen, etc.).

 Is your lecture hall equipped as electronic teaching room containing a computer, a projector CD/DVD player, Internet access, and a visual presenter? If so, arrange for training in the use of all of the equipment provided.

You should also make certain that the appropriate software is on the computer to run your program. More than once I have checked everything else worked before a lecture or presentation only to find that the correct software was not on the computer to run one of my programs. One of the most useful pieces of equipment in large lecture rooms is the visual presenter. This piece of equipment does away with the need to produce overhead transparencies.

With one of these electronic cameras you can project directly from the typed page without the additional step of producing costly overheads. Since the camera can also zoom in and out, one can even project directly from the printed page in a textbook or journal and use the zoom to magnify the image. I have even projected 35 mm color slides (rapidly becoming another obsolete technology) using the camera. Most instructors use PowerPoint (or an equivalent software package) to project their notes, pictures and graphics, and I have written about the good and poor uses of such types of presentation software with large classes in Chapter Four, "Technology in the Classroom," page 64.

Administration

Large classes can also be very time-consuming due simply to the large number of people in the class. For example, in a small class of, say 40 students, you could hand back marked tests and assignments by calling out the names of each of the students and passing out the relevant papers. Try handing back 200 papers that way! It would take most, if not all, of the class period just to hand back the papers. So how best to deal with collecting and distributing tests and assignments?

Ask student to place completed papers in piles marked in alphabetical order. Return the marked papers in a similar fashion, asking the students to come and pick up their papers at the end of the class.

Don't hand back tests or papers during your teaching time in class. Students will be distracted by the materials.

Lewis (1994) suggests that the following areas are ones in which an instructor may wish to consider streamlining:

1. Developing and duplicating handouts, exams and homework problems;

2. Handling out and collecting those handouts, exams, and homework problems;

3. Grading homework and exams;

4. Keeping track of several hundred student grades;

5. Providing timely feedback to students;

6. Getting questions from students and providing them with answers;

7. Managing office hours.

Teaching

Teaching a large class in a lecture theatre can bring problems of interactivity with students. Yazedjian and Kolkhorst point (2007) point out that, "Students who believe they are anonymous often feel less personally responsible for learning, are less motivated to learn, and are less likely to attend class (Cooper and Robinson

2000)." Lewis (1994) writes that, "Because large classes provide a great deal of anonymity, students frequently feel that they can talk to their neighbors, come or leave when they feel like it, and so forth, without suffering any kind of consequences."

Lewis suggests that instructors make a statement about their expectations of the students and their responsibilities to themselves and to their fellow classmates. Sometimes, students feel that the back of a large lecture theatre is a place to sit and chat with friends, or even a convenient place to have lunch when they are not even taking the course. Some lecture theatres I have visited can be so noisy that it is almost impossible to hear the instructor.

Much of the problem of uninvolved students is the teaching method employed in the circumstances. While this book does describe a number of different instructional strategies a number of them are not the easiest to employ in a large class situation. Almost inevitably, then, the lecture is the instructional method most usually employed with large classes.

 But if one is lecturing a large class, how does one make students interested, and hold their interest? Enthusiasm for your teaching and for your subject is the key.

As Weaver and Cottrell (1987) note, "If there is one instructor characteristic related to learning it is enthusiasm....The simplest person, fired with enthusiasm, is more persuasive than the most eloquent person without it."

If you are going to hold students' attention, it is important to vary the presentation. Interspersing a lecture with audiovisual materials, demonstrations, and short student activities all help to keep students' attention.

As I've pointed out before, a two-minute pause every 12-15 minutes or so, is a good way of restoring student energy, allowing the students a break from writing, and gives them an opportunity of reviewing their notes and discussing them with their classmates. Interspersing the lecture with a variety of student-based activities is important in any teaching situation, but is especially important in large classes.

The chapter titled "Alternative Instructional Strategies," page 104, describes a number of different strategies—most of which can be employed in large class situations. (You should also look at the chapter on "Improving the Lecture," page 115, for more hints). You should have a number of other activities ready to use at different times of the semester, but if you are new to teaching you should develop a few to try out, and each semester add new ones so that you eventually have quite a few to use as circumstances permit.

The easiest ones to try are these three:

• short demonstrations (especially if you have a student or two to assist you)

• setting problems for students to solve individually or in groups

• small group discussions to answer questions you pose

Remember that if you don't have such an activity to use in a particular lecture period, you can always employ the two-minute pause, making the purpose of the pause clear to the students.

In a large class, remember that the class is probably very heterogeneous and has a wide variety of learning styles. Try to address all the learning styles during the course of a lecture. Thus, in addition to talking—which addresses the aural learning style— make use of visuals such as overheads, PowerPoint slides, models etc. to address the needs of visual learners. Kinesthetic learners are more difficult to accommodate in a large class situation, since they need to handle items and move around. Strategies that involve them in demonstrations are important. Of course laboratory sessions are also well adapted for kinesthetic students' learning styles.

Communications

Since students in large classes are less likely to want to make comments or ask questions in front of their peers, the instructor may have to elicit communication with his/her students in a variety of ways.

One way is to ask students to form small groups to discuss a question posed to the class and then to ask groups to give an answer. While it is not feasible to ask every group for an answer, you will receive a fair number of answers as students, in the group format, may be more willing to speak in the larger classes. This question/answer strategy can be used throughout the semester, and as it becomes a familiar activity more groups will be prepared to offer answers. You can get almost instantaneous feedback from students with electronic "clickers," or non-technological versions such as cardboard cubes with different responses on each side, or even colored cards (with different colors on the two sides). Clickers are described in Chapter Four, "Technology in the Classroom," page 64.

Another interesting idea from Lewis (1994) is the use of question boxes placed near the door(s) in which students can place their written questions or comments, and which the instructor can answer in the next class. Of course there are a variety of technology-based options for students to ask questions, make comments and the like including e-mail, web forums, blogs, Twitter etc., all of which are also covered in the "Technology in the Classroom" chapter.

Other simple feedback options include the one-minute paper and the class questionnaire. Lewis (1994) suggests the one-minute paper given at the end of class asks the students to answer two short questions:

1. "What was the most important idea you learned during today's class?"

2. "What questions do you still have about the material discussed today?"

Another option, the brief questionnaire, takes students about five minutes to complete, and provides feedback about a single class.

Student response groups—a small group of students with whom the instructor meets every two weeks—is another tool that may be used. Other class members are encouraged to pass on their comments to the response group. You can even have informal open coffee sessions. Invite students to have coffee, and discuss the course with you.

Tests and Assignments

Clearly, testing and marking written assignments for large classes can be a challenge. In another chapter I'll discuss a number of ideas which can be of immense help in a large class, but it is worth mentioning some of them again here:

1. Use a number of tests/exams but don't count all of them in calculating a student's final mark. Under this scheme, students can drop a low score, or can miss a test without you having to give *any* make-up exams.

2. Have a protocol/policy in place to deal with students asking for re-reads of papers, and stick to it.

3. Written assignments do not have to be onerously long. Assign 1000-word writing projects and/or micro-themes.

4. Use an assignment hand-out. Not only does it make marking much easier, but it also reduces significantly the numbers of students asking for re-marks since they can see from the attachment where their strong and weak points are.

5. If you have the use of TA's (teaching assistants) do not use them for grading subjective responses on tests and assignments – it will result in too much variability in grading standards. Use them to mark the more content-style questions. You should be the one to grade written assignments and essay questions.

Teaching Assistants

You may be lucky enough to be assigned TA's to help in large classes. So how best to make use of TA's? I primarily use TA's to help in proctoring exams and grading those exams, but I have also used them, depending on their background and experience, to assist in teaching (if I am away), holding office hours (in addition to mine), and even running tutorials and remedial or revision classes. It is always important to meet with them as a group first to explain how you intend to make use of them, and the way you would like them to work with you and the class.

For grading tests, I give each of them a copy of the answer sheet in advance, and ask them to mark a few papers the first evening after a test, and ask each of them to call me at home, or contact me by e-mail, if they have any concerns. Any questions are answers and problems solved before too many of the tests are completely graded. I may even gather them together the next day so that we can all go through the graded exams, and make any necessary adjustments.

A Final Comment

 Remember that teaching large classes can be fun and exhilarating.

I find teaching very small classes much more challenging than teaching larger ones. Heppner, in *Teaching the Large College Class* (2007), writes, "Teaching large classes well is the most difficult and challenging task in academia and offers the fewest tangible rewards. Knowing, however, that you have a real, positive, and inspiring effect on hundreds or thousands of young people will more than compensate for the liabilities. Do it right and you will have former students all over the world who will be grateful to you for the wisdom you gave them."

Figure 5.1

"We've raised the student cap."

CHAPTER 6
WHO ARE OUR STUDENTS?

The Millennial Student

The students arriving at colleges and universities today are very different from those of former years. Students today are probably the most heterogeneous of any post-secondary education generation, and today's classes are made up of a wider variety of ages than in the past—when the majority were recent high school graduates. A number of our students may have worked for a number of years before coming to university/college and bring, therefore, a wide range of work experiences with them. The classes today also represent a wider diversity of ethnic backgrounds than ever before, and increasingly, greater numbers of international students.

The majority of our students, however, will belong to the new generation of students, often dubbed Millenials (born after 1981), who are quite different from the previous generations of students (Baby Boomers, Gen Xers, etc.). What is it about these Millennial students that requires university and college instructors to modify their teaching strategies? If there is one thing that differentiates Millennial students from previous generations of students it has to be their familiarity with, and dependence, on technology.

You need walk the corridors of post-secondary institutions to realize the importance of technology in students' lives, whether it be MP3 players, iPods, iPads, iPhones, Blackberries, cell phones or laptop computers. However, not only are today's students fully conversant with these technologies, they use them simultaneously, and want to be connected (electronically) on a continuous basis.

Who Are Our Students?

Many of today's students also hold the equivalent of full-time jobs, on or off-campus, often working evening jobs thereby reducing the amount of time they have available for study. So, as instructors, how do we teach these students to best recognize their strengths and weaknesses?

 Clearly, their familiarity with technology and multi-tasking, together with their need for instant gratification, don't mesh well with the standard lecture approach to teaching which treats students as passive learners.

According to Terry O'Banion (1997), "Colleges and universities will find a generation that will simply not put up with traditional lecture formats and professors who teach in the 'great person' traditions. Rather, the next generation of students will be demanding consumers who expect active engagement in the learning process."

Clearly, to fully engage such students requires us to utilize more active teaching and learning methods, and to incorporate the use of technology with which these students are all too familiar.

Lessons From Tobias's "Second Tier" Study

In her study of the so-called "Second Tier" students, Tobias (1990) recruited a number of non-science students to take introductory courses in Chemistry and Physics to find out whether they could be converted into science majors. One of these students, Eric (an Arts major), took an introductory Physics course. He found that the course demanded considerably more time than he had ever spent in his literature studies. Many of his (science or physics major) classmates were taking six or seven hours a day to do the work. Eric noted that, "Aside from the pure misery of devoting that much of your life to physics, I wonder how much they, or rather we, will retain."

When Eric asked himself "what makes science hard?" he came to the conclusion that students will perceive a course to be 'hard' when it is:

1) difficult to get a good grade;

2) time consuming; or

3) boring, dull or simply not fun.

Unfortunately Eric found Physics to be all of the above. Tobias concluded that, "Something besides the traditional problem-solving approach may be needed to excite new students to physics. But at least as important as content, if Eric's reactions are typical, will be changes in the "classroom culture" of physical science: more attention to an intellectual overview, more context (even history) in the presentation of physical models, less condescending pedagogy, differently challenging examinations, and, above all, more discussion, more "dissent" (even if artificially constructed), and more "community" in the classroom."

 Tobias writes a key finding is that, "....the college science classroom is perceived by most women, whether they succeed at and persist in science or not, as an "unfriendly place to be. More than their male classmates, women appear to be "uncomfortable working in the intensely competitive environment" that characterizes many introductory science classes."

Tobias speculates that this "unease" may contribute to the higher attrition rate among women considering a science major. The conclusion is that certain students, among them women and, most likely, our second tiers, would respond better to science, if more "cooperative and interactive modes of learning" were part of the pedagogy, and if, scientific knowledge were more closely and explicitly linked to important societal issues."

Tobias's study, therefore, clearly indicates that at least in the physical sciences, we need to adopt more student-active teaching strategies, and to note the importance of connecting the content to societal issues. While Tobias's study related to the "second tiers" the lessons can equally be applied to the science majors.

Student Learning Styles

Instructors are apt to teach all the students in a class as if they were all alike, and, therefore, learn in the same way, but the research literature clearly shows that different students learn in very different ways depending on factors such as their learning modality preference, learning styles, and even their personalities.

Samples (1994), for instance, distinguishes between four different learning modalities, namely, visual-spatial, auditory, kinesthetic, and symbolic-abstract.

"Each person develops preferences among the sensory modes favored for learning. For example, a student with visual-spatial preferences will tend to rely on sight as the favored sense for accessing information and experience. Students with an auditory preference will tend to focus on hearing and the patterning of sound, Kinesthetic students will seek out learning that focuses on touch, movement, and full body participation."

These three learning modalities are commonly encountered in the literature, but Samples (1994) adds a fourth.

"There is also a modality that I call symbolic abstract. This is not a sensory modality as much as it is a modality of brain design. Parts of the left cortex seem predisposed to use symbols to interpret the forms of expression we call reading, writing and the mathematical symbols."

In addition to learning modalities the literature also shows that students are characterized by different learning styles. But why is it important to be aware of different learning styles? Felder (1993) says that, "Students whose learning styles are compatible with the teaching style of a course instructor tend to retain information longer, apply it more effectively, and have more positive post-course attitudes toward the subject than do their counterparts who experience learning/teaching style mismatches."

Felder and Silverman (1988) have formulated a learning style model that is applicable to science instruction and which distinguishes five different learning style dimensions:

1. **Sensing/Intuitive** — The type of information the student prefers to receive. — sensory (sights, sounds, physical sensations) intuitive (memories, ideas, insights).

2. **Visual/Verbal** — The modality through which sensory information is most effectively perceived. —visual (pictures, diagrams, graphs, demonstrations), verbal (sounds, written and spoken words).

3. **Inductive/Deductive** — The organization of information with which the student is most comfortable— inductive (facts and observations are given, and underlying principles are inferred), deductive (principles are given, and consequences and applications are induced).

4. **Active/Reflective** — The student's preference for processing information — actively (through engagement in discussion or physical activity), reflectively (through introspection).

5. **Sequential/Global** — The student's progress towards understanding — sequentially (in a logical progression of small steps), globally (holistically, in large jumps).

Each of these learning style dimension pairs are continuous and not either/or categories. Felder (1993) writes that, "A student's preference on a given scale may be strong, moderate, or almost non-existent, may change with time, and may vary from one subject or learning environment to another."

Felder writes that most of the points raised by Tobias about the poor quality of introductory college science instruction are failures to address certain common learning styles.

Felder (1993) points out that: "Most people (at least in Western cultures) and presumably most students in science classes are visual learners (Barbe and Milone 1981), while the information presented in almost every lecture course is overwhelmingly verbal – written words and formulas in texts and on the chalkboard, spoken words in lectures, with only an occasional diagram, chart or demonstration breaking the pattern."

Felder goes on to explain: "The teaching style in most lecture courses tilts heavily toward the small percentage of college students who are intuitive, verbal, deductive, reflective, and sequential. This imbalance puts a sizeable fraction of the student population at a disadvantage."

These mismatches between teaching styles in most science courses and student learning styles have serious consequences.

"Students ....feel as if they are being in an unfamiliar foreign language: they tend to get lower grades than students whose learning styles are better matched to the instructor's teaching style (Godleski, 1984), and are less likely to develop an interest in the course material (Felder, 1988)."

Felder concludes that sensing, visual, inductive, active and global learners rarely have their educational needs met in science courses. Such mismatches between the teaching style of the professor and the preferred learning style of the student can result in lower grades, less interest in the subject, and even a loss of interest in science altogether. Maybe then, one of the reasons why so many students switch from the sciences to other fields after their first-year at college or university is because of the mismatch between instructor teaching style and student learning styles.

Clearly it is impossible to change our teaching styles to match the learning style of each of our students, but it is possible to adapt our teaching styles. Felder (1993) suggests that a reasonable balance could be achieved if we were to address each type of learning style dimension at least some of the time. He says that of the ten learning style categories, five (intuitive, verbal, deductive, reflective and sequential), are already adequately covered by the traditional lecture approach. In order to adequately address the other learning styles Felder suggests the following:

1. Balance concrete information (e.g., results from real experiments **[sensing]**) with conceptual information (e.g., theories, models etc. **[intuitive]**).

2. Make extensive use of sketches, plots, schematics, physical demonstrations etc. **[visual]** in addition to oral and written explanations and derivations **[verbal]**.

3. Use physical analogies and demonstrations to illustrate the magnitudes of calculated quantities **[sensing, global]** i.e., 100 microns – that's about the thickness of a sheet of paper. i.e., "100 microns – that's about the thickness of a sheet of paper."

4. Provide time in class for students to think about the material being presented **[reflective]** and for active student participation **[active]**.

5. To illustrate abstract concepts or problem-solving algorhythms, use at least some numerical examples **[sensing]** to supplement the usual algebraic examples **[intuitive]**.

6. Give some experimental observations before presenting the general principles and have the students (preferably working in groups) see how far they can get toward inferring the latter **[inductive]**.

7. Encourage or mandate cooperation on assignments **[active]**.

8. Demonstrate the logical flow of individual course topics [**sequential**], but also point out connections between the current material and other relevant material in the same course, in other courses in the same discipline, in other disciplines, and in everyday experience [**global**].

We sometimes find it difficult to appreciate that not everyone learns in the same way, but we have to realize that other people's ways of learning is not wrong, it's just different.

A number of studies have indicated that achievement in university/college courses is also linked to a student's personality as measured on the Myers-Briggs Type Indicator (MBTI). We will look at the effect of personality on achievement in the next chapter as it seems that science majors and non-majors differ in personality traits.

Piaget's Theory of Intellectual Development

While Piaget's theory, originally developed in the early part of the last century, has been modified by subsequent researchers and even discounted by others, enough articles have examined its implications for science teaching to make it one of the most significant theories to impact the teaching of college-level science, particularly at the introductory level.

Piaget's research shows that intellectual development results from the interaction between an organism and its environment, and his observations on Swiss children led to the identification of four principal stages in cognitive development as shown below.

1. Sensorimotor intelligence   (0-2 years)

2. Pre-operational thought   (2-7 years)

3. Concrete operational thought   (7-11 years)

4. Formal operational thought   (11-15 years)

How is Piaget's work relevant at the college level? It is now recognized that Piaget's suggested ages for each stage are not universal, and there is a fair body of evidence that many college-level students are still operating at the concrete operational stage. According to Kolodiy (1974), "The main difference between this stage (concrete) and the final one of formal operations is that the concrete operational child cannot deal with hypothetical problems or those involving the future .... The child at the formal level can deal with all kinds of problems – present, past, future, or hypo-thetical. He can apply reasoning and hypothesis building."

 While it is generally agreed that introductory science courses, especially those in phys-ics, require thinking at the formal level of operational thought, studies have consistently shown that significant numbers of students in these courses have not yet reached this level of thinking.

How then do we modify our teaching methods so as to ensure that we are reaching all of our students, both at the "concrete" and "formal" levels of operational thought, and particularly in introductory courses? As an example let us look at teaching the concept of diffusion.

For "formal" level students, who can deal in abstractions, we could describe it in words and diagrams on a chalkboard, but for "concrete" level students, we should incorporate demonstrations or hands-on activities so that they can see for themselves rather than having to visualize the process. For instance, a simple but effective demonstration of diffusion is to release a perfume or similar scent (provided of course that none of the students have allergies to perfumes or scents) at the front of the room, and ask students to raise their hands when they detect the perfume. One can also calculate the speed of diffusion.

Such relatively simple activities and demonstrations within the body of the lecture may take longer to complete than regular lectures but they are much more meaningful to the 'concrete' learners who may well comprise over half of our introductory classes.

Six Quick Tips For Teaching Millennials

1. Many of our students are so-called "millennial" students who are heavy users of technology so it is a good idea to incorporate the use of such technologies in your teaching.

2. Students are more heterogeneous than before with more minority students, international students, and mature students present, so it is important to be inclusive of all of them.

3. Students vary in their learning styles, so it is important to adapt one's teaching to a wider range of learning styles. Include visuals and demonstrations in addition to straight lecturing, and also include some class activities (problem solving, group discussions, etc.) which allow students to interact and socialize with each other. This is especially important for non-major's courses since these students can have very different learning styles to science majors.

4. Classrooms should be more friendly and less competitive.

5. Research on personality types also shows that different personalities like to learn in different ways and the different sciences seem to attract different personality traits.

6. Remember that, particularly in introductory courses, many of the students may still be in the concrete level of operational thought so that is important to incorporate 'concrete' demonstrations and activities which will help these learners better understand abstract concepts.

CHAPTER 7
TEACHING NON-SCIENCE MAJORS

Often students not majoring in science have to take courses designed for the science major. Many instructors and administrators would argue that all students should take the same course(s), while others would argue that with shrinking funding, science departments should allocate their precious resources to the offering of courses to their own majors. This seems to me to be a short-sighted view of whom we should be teaching. The teaching of courses to non-majors is at least as important as teaching the science majors!

If we, as instructors, can convince these non-majors of the importance of science to them as individuals, and to society at large, and the importance of scientific research, then we invest in the security of our own scientific futures. In fact, there are many reasons for improving the scientific literacy of all members of society.

Another argument for the importance of science courses to non-majors is that perhaps some of them might consider switching their majors to science, an important consideration at a time when we are facing a shortfall in the number of scientists needed in the U.S. While as many as half a million students take introductory college science each year, many of these will drop the study of science after their first year, and even fewer will graduate with a science degree. Clearly, many of our brightest students are being turned off by poor science instruction (Lipson and Tobias 1991).

Larson (1982) contends that science courses are often bogged down with jargon, symbols, arithmetic metaphors and analytical processes which can discourage non-majors. Nastase and Scharmann (1991) write that science instructors make the assumption that students share their enthusiasm for science in general, whereas it has been demonstrated that significant numbers of college students believe the sciences have very little to do with their personal lives (Ewing, Campbell and Brown, 1987). Whether we teach non-science majors in separate courses, or in courses primarily designed for scientists, the question to be answered is how best we can do this knowing that non-majors differ in a number of ways from science majors, including having an aversion to jargon, and feeling that science has very little to do with their own personal lives?

Myers-Briggs Indicator

As it turns out, there is lots of information about the differences between science majors and non-science majors which can inform us as how best to teach non-majors, whether they are in a non-majors course or are in a majors course together with science majors. A number of researchers have examined the relationship between personality, choice of discipline, and achievement. McCauley (1977), in a study of entering students at the University of Florida, used the Myers-Briggs Indicator (MBTI) to examine personality types and choices of major. The MBTI identifies individuals along four dichotomous scales as shown below:

- E-I (Extraversion-Introversion): Is the person interested in the outer world of people and action or the inner world of ideas and concepts?

- S-N (Sensing-Intuition): Does the person perceive the real, practical facts of life with their senses or use intuition, imagination, and inspiration to see the possibilities and meanings beyond facts?

- T-F (Thinking-Feeling): Does the person make judgments or decisions objectively and impersonally based on facts and logic or are decisions made subjectively and personally, relying on empathy and feelings?

- J-P (Judgment-Perception): Does the person prefer to live in a decisive, planned, and orderly way or in a spontaneous, flexible manner?

McCauley found that the different personality types were attracted to different discipline as shown below:

Personality Type	Major
NT	physical sciences, engineering
SF	nursing, education
ST	biological sciences
NF, EN	humanities, behavioral science
ES	physical ed., nursing, business

Melear (1990) found the typical non-major could be described as ESFP, whereas the science majors were generally of the INTJ type. So it does appear that the personality types of non-majors differ from those of science majors. For the most part, incorporating a number of student-based activities in our teaching (i.e., small group work, discussion situations, cooperative learning, and alternative assignments such as portfolios) would enable non-majors to become more involved in science classes.

We need to establish the relevance of science to students' individual lives and personal interests, to allow students to become more actively involved in their own learning, and to incorporate cooperative learning situations in the classroom, rather then emphasizing the competition for grades.

Teaching Strategies

Obviously we can't find out the learning styles of every student in the class, and then adjust our teaching. Felder (1993) says we should address each side of each learning style dimension at least some of the time. He says that of the ten defined learning style categories (intuitive, verbal, deductive, reflective, and sequential) are adequately covered by the traditional lecture-based teaching approach. There are other teaching strategies that address those five learning style dimensions not adequately covered in the traditional lecture (sensing, visual, inductive, active and global).

It's important to incorporate a number of different teaching strategies to appeal to a wide variety of student learning styles. For instance, while the lecture is a main teaching strategy, also use visuals, including photographs, magazine articles, cell models and the like, as well as PowerPoint slides. Pose a few questions/problems, ask groups of students to discuss, and ask a number of groups for answers. Maintain a Web forum for students to discuss issues related to the course, so the inductive, active and global learners may be actively involved in the course.

Reduce unnecessary reliance on terminology. Rowe (1982) has pointed out that students in first-year chemistry courses may be expected to assimilate 6,000-6,750 units of information, more new language than is found in the first year of foreign language study, and in chemistry the meanings as well as the words are new. Rowe also says that lecturers commonly add ideas, as much as 20 percent more new material not found in the textbook.

While it may be argued that it is essential to learn this material in order to be successful in higher courses, this obviously does not apply to non-majors who may never take another science course. If you are teaching non-majors in a class more specifically designed for majors, it may not be that easy to eliminate much scientific jargon without causing the majors potential problems in more senior courses. However, by introducing instructional strategies more oriented to non-majors, it should be possible to cover the learning styles, personalities, and interests of both science majors and non-majors.

CHAPTER 8
TO LECTURE OR NOT TO LECTURE?

According to Bligh (2000), so ingrained is the lecture in higher education, that over 95 percent of science professors in the U.S. use it as their main teaching method, and this in spite of all the research showing that students do not learn well in lecture situations.

 A study at the University of California at Berkeley (Angelo, 1991) has shown that college students only remember 20 percent of what they hear from a traditional lecture or demonstration several days after the class. Furthermore, this study also found that, in a room full of dozens of students, fewer than 15 percent are paying attention to what is being presented at any one time during the class, not counting the first eight minutes of a class when a much higher percentage of students are following the lecture.

Thus, the major reason for this is that students do not expend much energy thinking about what is being discussed in a traditional-style presentation. Students may also be so busy writing notes that they don't have the time to think about what they are actually doing.

It reminds me of a cartoon I have, showing a student returning home from school and telling his father, "They don't give us time to learn anything; we have to listen to the teacher all day." How very true. This does not mean that we should suddenly abandon lectures to teach but make the best use of the time we have in a class to ensure students are actually learning. Otherwise, we might find that the following quote is all too true: "With the lecture, the information usually passes from the notes of the instructor to the notes of the students without passing through the minds of either!"

One thing that greatly influenced my own teaching when I became aware of it was the issue of student attention span in the *What's the Use of Lectures* book by Bligh (1971). One graph in his book shows the typical decrement curve for a person's attention to a single task over a period of time.

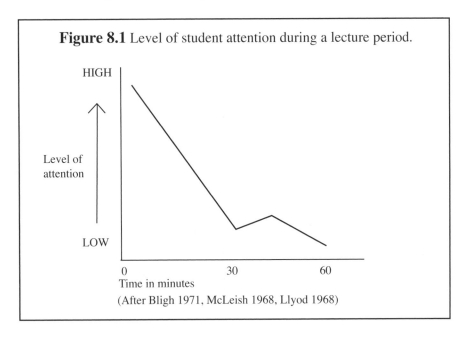

Figure 8.1 Level of student attention during a lecture period.

HIGH

Level of attention

LOW

0   30   60

Time in minutes

(After Bligh 1971, McLeish 1968, Llyod 1968)

This pattern is usually displayed in the level of performance of students during a lecture. It has been suggested (McLeish 1968; Lloyd 1968) that student attention rises and falls in the last five minutes of a 55 minute lecture. Not surprisingly the student level of attention is highest at the start of a lecture but begins to decline thereafter, and around 10-20 minutes into the lecture the level of attention begins to decrease dramatically and continues to decline for the rest of the hour until the last five minutes. In fact student attention has been shown to drop off after only 10 to 15 minutes (Hartley and Davies, 1978). This suggests that the attention span of an average student might only be around 10-15 minutes during which time the most learning takes place.

Bligh (1971) notes that several studies have found a marked improvement in attention after a short break. The second graph below shows the effect of a rest or change of activity on the level of attention after a break of a few minutes. If there is such a rest period for a few minutes, when the lecture resumes, the amount of effective learning is almost as high as it was at the start of the lecture. Again, the amount of effective learning will drop off during the next part of the lecture.

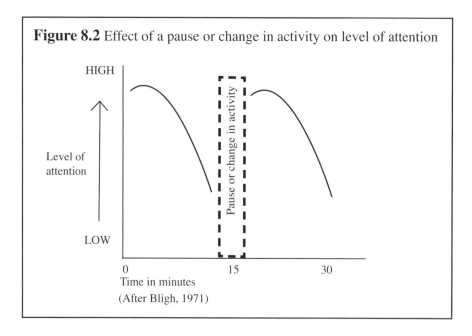

Figure 8.2 Effect of a pause or change in activity on level of attention

A number of studies have examined the efficacy of pauses during a one-hour lecture period, and these all confirm that students are more attentive during the lecture period, and do better on subsequent tests.

Ruhl et al. (2007) point out that the pause may also benefit the lecturer since he/she may use the pauses to scan the lecture notes and, perhaps, improve the quality of his/her delivery after the pause.

Try it out for yourself! Inform your class that you will teach for 15 minutes and then take a two-minute break. During this break students should review their notes to see if there was anything they didn't understand, and discuss it with a neighbor to see if the neighbor could explain it to them. If not, the student can ask questions on the material after the break. The two-minute break allows students to socialize with, and get to know their neighbors, and will give you a few minutes to get organized for the next part of the lecture.

Several years ago, to try out the strategy I used the two-minute pause with a single class during an entire semester, and when the grades for all the sections were tallied at the end of term, that section performed significantly better than all the others. And why wouldn't they? I had taught in smaller chunks of time when student learning was most effective, and students could discuss problems with each other during the pauses.

Since that initial trial run, I've continued to use this technique when lecturing.

 When talking to colleagues about my use of this technique, they often comment that I have *lost* four minutes of instructional time in a fifty-minute lecture! Of course, what is most important is not the *quantity* of teaching time, but the *quality* of the student learning.

It is important to point out that Bligh's graph points to a change of activity after approximately 12-14 minutes. It follows from what we discussed in previous chapters, that good science teachers employ more active techniques to allow students to become better involved in their own learning. Such activities might include solving problems you present to the class, small group discussions, demonstrations, and a variety of other techniques dealt with later in this book.

It is perhaps also worth noting that Bligh (1971) reports that the rate of decrement (i.e., loss of attention) is steeper for more difficult subject matter and, therefore, the more difficult the lecture material the more frequent the pauses or variations in teaching should be. Bligh also points out that the same decrements in attention occur during the course of a day.

While some people reach their optimum level of performance during the morning, and others at midday, very few people are at their best in the afternoon. Thus, attention to lectures is more difficult in the afternoon and evening, lectures delivered at those times should be shorter, more varied, and more stimulating, should give way to small group teaching and other active methods of learning.

Figure 8.3

First Time Teacher Revelation #27

CHAPTER 9
ALTERNATIVE INSTRUCTIONAL STRATEGIES

In this chapter, we will examine some alternative but well-tried and tested approaches to teaching and learning. Don't regard any one technique as *the* one you should use at the expense of the others, but think of situations in which you could use them from time-to-time. If you are using lectures as your main method of teaching, think of a few situations in which you can introduce a variety of strategies to sample during the course of a semester. Introducing a few new and different approaches in your teaching will greatly increase student interest.

The Learning Cycle in the Science Classroom

A learning cycle reverses the usual "lecture followed by laboratory" sequence—the lecture phase comes later in the process, and not at the beginning. This technique has broad applicability at the college/university level.

The typical learning cycle includes three phases: exploration, term introduction, and finally concept application. "During exploration, students learn through their own actions and reactions in a new situation. In this phase they often explore a new phenomenon with minimal guidance.

"... The second phase, term introduction, normally starts with the introduction of a new term or terms ... used to label the pattern discovered during exploration. ... In the last phase of the learning cycle, concept application, students apply the new term and/or reasoning pattern to additional examples." (Lawson, 1988).

My first introduction to this type of strategy was an earth sciences activity and it struck me that this was a very worthwhile strategy to use in my own subject, biology, but at the time I couldn't think of how to immediately apply it in my own teaching. An opportunity arose a short time later when I was asked by a colleague teaching an invertebrate biology course to give a guest lecture on the group of invertebrates I researched, the Phylum Tardigrada (water bears). Rather than give a traditional lecture, I decided to try the Learning Cycle approach, even though it was a large class of 225.

At the beginning of the class I projected a diagram with drawings of eight different tardigrades, together with their sizes, and asked the class to get into small groups (2-3) and using the diagrams to work out what they thought might be the major characteristics of the group. I gave the class ten minutes for this activity. I then asked one group to give me one characteristic which I then wrote on the board, and then did the same for a number of other groups. I then asked if anyone else had other characteristics to add to the list. I then went through the list one by one to see if everyone agreed. This led to some spirited discussions of some of the characteristics identified so far. This phase constitutes the 'Exploration Phase.'

In the second phase "Term Introduction" I then gave the 'correct' characteristics of the group and gave the correct biological term for each of the characteristics (e.g., bilateral symmetry, pharynx, placoids etc.) identified by the students.

In the final phase, "Concept Application", I gave each group of students drawings of two further organisms, which might or might not be tardigrades, and asked them to decide, with reasons, whether or not each was a tardigrade. This also generated very lively discussions, with some very heated group arguments!

After five minutes or so I then projected each drawing in turn, asking the groups with those drawings for their decision, with their reasoning. Once the groups had their say I then invited the rest of the class to comment, which again led to some 'heated' debates.

This particular exercise was so successful that I have used it with other invertebrate Biology classes, and in Education courses, and even years later students remembered that particular activity, so it obviously made an impression!

While I have no data to support the contention that students learn better using this approach, informally I have been told by students time and time again that they will always remember tardigrades! I have even used the activity at higher education conferences and had participants at these sessions meet me several years later and say that they still remembered tardigrades, and most of these were non-scientists. The 'learning cycle' then is an alternative to the usual lecture format which is a very student interactive strategy and which can be used from time-to-time in a variety of science classes, and is particularly useful in large class situations.

Cooperative Learning

"Cooperative learning may be defined as a classroom learning environment in which students work together in heterogeneous groups towards completion of a common goal" (Watson and Marshall, 1995).

Cooperative, or collaborative, learning is a technique which is widely used in schools but infrequently in colleges and universities. While there are very few references to the use of this technique at the college/university level, there is, nonetheless, an enormous amount of research in the literature which demonstrates its effectiveness. Watson and Marshall (1995) say that this technique may be especially important in science teaching since laboratory instruction often includes the grouping of students, and since the actual practice of science involves collaborating with one another.

Caprio (1993) states that there are many affective and cognitive gains which can be realized from the use of cooperative learning.

"Those most closely related to motivation include the enhancement of self-esteem, the social and academic support acquired from the personal study groups frequently originate, and the sense of belonging they engender in their members."

Caprio goes on to write that, "Engaging science in this personal context can form positive associations and attitudes to the subject and motivate further learning."

Watson (1992) lists a number of types of cooperative learning methods including:

---

1. Jigsaw approach

Each student in a group is given a topic on which to become an 'expert'. Each student from a group meets with the 'experts' on the same topic from other groups. The 'expert' then relays his/her knowledge back to the rest of the group. Students are tested individually on the material.

2. Student teams (Achievement divisions)

The instructor prepares a lesson and students study worksheets, test each other, and then are tested individually. These results are combined into team scores.

3. Team games and tournaments

This is similar to 2, but at the end of the unit there is a group competition for team scores.

4. Learning together

Groups of students study a topic and produce a worksheet or test, which is then the basis for evaluating the groups. Students are also evaluated individually.

5. Coop

Teams of students choose topics to study and then divide them into subtopics, with each individual responsible for learning and teaching a subtopic. The team then makes a presentation on the topic to the whole class.

6. Group investigation

Each group chooses a general topic to study. Individuals or pairs of students then study the subtopics. The group then makes a presentation on the topic to the whole class.

Cooperative learning is easier to use in smaller class settings. As an example, I have taught the different biomes using the Jigsaw method rather than by lectures. If you choose, say, three biomes — tundra, taiga and deciduous forest — groups of three students would each become responsible for learning about each biome, using materials you provide. The student "expert" on each biome then meets with "experts" on the same biome from other groups. When each of these biome "super-groups" has decided on the main characteristics of each biome (climate, geographical location, weather, main animals and plants), each expert goes back to his/her group to teach the others about that biome. The class can end in a test to see how well each student has learnt about each biome. It can be made into a team competition by either adding up the marks of each team member, or by having the whole team answer the questions together.

Problem-Based Learning (PLB)

Problem-based learning is a technique often used in smaller upper-undergraduate classes. It was originally pioneered at McMaster University's School of Medicine in the 1970s, and has been widely used. Instead of learning basic information and only applying it later in more advanced courses, PBL focuses, in Medicine, on a particular medical patient case and in the resulting investigation the students find the factual information that bears on the case. (The television program "House" is a good example of the technique.) At the start of a session, students are given a problem to solve and work in small groups to come up with the solution. Herreid (2003) describes a typical scenario:

"On the first day they receive a new case: a story about a patient with a set of symptoms and some clinical tests results. Sometimes they actually see the patient in the flesh or on video. The students, with reference books in hand, analyze the case to determine as best as they can what the trouble with the patient might be."

A tutor helps the group decide what the issues are and what they will need to find out to solve the case. This process usually lasts for one week and students subdivide the workload among themselves. In the final class the students pool their knowledge, complete their diagnosis, and plan a final report.

Since the early use of PBL in medical schools, this strategy has also been applied to undergraduate courses in biology, chemistry and physics. Given the amount of work required of faculty, it is not a technique that lends itself to use in large, undergraduate courses, but instead is better suited to smaller, senior undergraduate classes.

Concept Maps

Novak (1993), the originator of the "concept map," says that the most important single factor influencing learning is what the learner already knows. In a long-term study Novak examined how children's concepts of the particle nature of matter changed over twelve years of schooling, and he identified three key factors:

1. Meaningful learning involves the assimilation of new concepts and propositions into existing cognitive structures;

2 Knowledge is organized hierarchically in cognitive structure, and most new learning involves subsumption of concepts and propositions into existing hierarchies; and

3. Knowledge acquired by rote learning will not be assimilated.

The "concept map" is a technique widely used in K-12 education, but only more recently at the college/university level. A concept map is a diagram that shows a number of key terms within a major concept, as well as the relationships between the terms. Wesley and Wesley (1990) give the following guidelines for constructing a concept map:

"General concepts should be at the top of the map, with the specific concepts arranged below in their degree of generation. The learning task itself determines the levels of a given concept map. In a typical map, concepts are written inside circles, ellipses, or boxes. Related concepts are connected by lines, and the nature of the relationship is denoted by connecting words that form propositions. Connections between concepts are linear as well as horizontal, so that a concept map is read from top to bottom and left to right as a sentence or series of sentences."

Ault (1985) says that the actual mapping process can be divided into five steps, namely select, rank, cluster, arrange and link. Okebukola (1990) in paraphrasing Ault's steps, divides the first step into two, selecting and choosing, as shown below:

1. Select an item for mapping. This could be an important text passage, lecture, notes or laboratory background material.

2. Choose and underline key words or phrases; include objects and events in the list.

3. Rank the concepts from the most abstract and inclusive to the most concrete and specific.

4. Cluster the concepts according to two criteria: concepts that function at a similar level of abstraction and concepts that inter-relate closely.

5. Arrange the concepts as a two-dimensional array analogous to a road map. Each concept is, in effect, a potential destination for understanding. Its route is defined by other concepts in the neighbouring territory.

6. Link related concepts with lines and label each line proposi-tional or prepositional form."

Ault's article is a good one to read for more information on the construction of concept maps as he shows how an example map (for Earth Science) is drawn up stage by stage. He recommends writing each of the original concepts on small cards for easy re-arrangement. I have used post-it notes instead of small cards as they have the advantage of sticking to an underlying base.

Figure 9.1 Concept Map

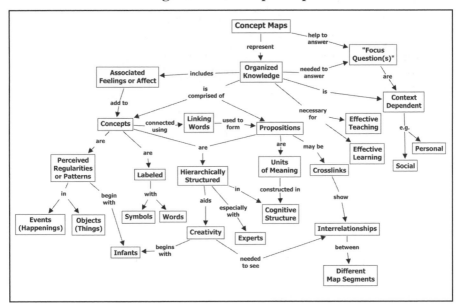

Meta-analyses have shown that concept mapping has raised student achievement by 0.46 standard deviations, or from the 50th to the 60th percentile (Horton et al., 1993). Roughly translated, this means that a student who would otherwise have scored 50 percent, would have scored 68 percent using concept mapping. The findings in Biology were even more impressive with students, on average, scoring at the 72nd percentile. In fact concept mapping seems to improve not only a student's academic achievement but also their attitude to the subject (Horton et. al., 1993). A teacher-prepared concept map can also function as an advance organizer, another Ausubelian instructional technique we will examine later in this book. Cliburn (1991), for instance writes that, "At the beginning of a unit, I present the whole unit concept map to the class using an overhead projector. I also often distribute copies of the maps to the students, and make sure to carefully explain them to the class. An oral presentation generally takes no more than 10 minutes of class time."

Case Studies

Case studies have been commonly used in law and business education for many years. According to Herreid (2003) the case study method started around the turn of the twentieth century in Harvard's law and business schools, with Harvard defining the method as students solving real cases with real dilemmas. Students were given a written case, were allowed time to analyze it, and then discussed the case in the classroom, examining the background for the problem and searching for alternative ways of solving it. Today, the case study approach is well-utilized in business and law programs, but not in science education.

Group Discussions

Another important instructional strategy is that of the group discussion. Students like to interact with each other, and this strategy allows plenty of opportunity for student interaction. Set a clear question or questions to be answered, and make sure that the problem is an open-ended one with no one clear answer. An example of such a group discussion problem I have used is this one:

"In a recent English study published in *Nature,* 30 people took 500 milligrams of Vitamin C for 6 weeks. Researchers took blood samples before, during and after the 6 week period to examine the DNA of white blood cells. They concluded that there were signs of genetic damage caused by free radicals due to the Vitamin C.

Discussion Question: What are the good and bad points of this study? What would you change to make this a better study?"

Students get 10 minutes to discuss this problem in small groups and then ask for first, the good points, and then the bad points, and list these on the chalkboard. Then I ask groups to suggest ways in which the study could be improved.

Context Creation

Later on in the book we will talk about student misconceptions and the problems they can cause in the effective learning of new material. Much of the research into student misconceptions, however, has focused on the students' learning processes and the learning content itself, while relatively little has been published on the teacher's actual teaching as a possible cause Van Rooyen (1994). A good teacher, therefore, is one whose teaching tries to avoid giving misconceptions.

"A teacher who is able to explain things in a clear and unambiguous way has less chance of contributing to misconceptions in the student's perception of those things" (Van Rooyen, 1994).

Van Rooyen argues that what he terms "context creation" represents a very important dimension of a teacher's ability to give clear explanations to students. The principle of context creation is that information presented to the students should be put into a context that students can readily understand, so that any likelihood of student misconception is reduced. Van Rooyen gives the example of a teacher wishing to give an indication of the relative size of the Class Insecta (850,000 species) in relation to the Kingdom Animalia and the Phylum Arthropoda. One could simply state the numbers but according to Van Rooyen, "... a large number of students simply will not be able to cognitively come to grips with these numbers and thus will not see the Insecta for what it is – a very dominant part of the animal Kingdom!"

He suggests the following alternative:

"Should one be able to organize a parade of the various Phyla of the animal Kingdom to that one representative of every known species appears on the scene every second, such a parade would take 12 days and 23 hours to cover the whole of the animal Kingdom. Of these almost 13 days, one would have to sit for 10 days and 16.5 hours only watching Arthropods, and the Insecta alone would take up 9 days and 20 hours. Beetles alone would occupy a full 2 days and 21.5 hours!" (Fretter and Graham, quoted by De Graaf, 1984).

I have taken this idea of context creation one step further and made it into a student activity. Part of one of my courses required a consideration of the number of species in each kingdom and phylum and as, van Rooyen stated, I could simply have listed the relevant numbers, but few students would have fully taken in the relative importance of the Arthropoda.

The class in question had 200 or more students, and I devised an activity in which I had each student represent a phylum or part thereof. Before the class started, I stood by the door and handed each student a 3" x 5" file card with a letter of the alphabet on it, but gave no indication as to what it was for. The students were intrigued, and interest in the class was clearly heightened. This is an example of a "hook" to get students interested in a class.

As I read out the letters in alphabetical order one or more students would come down to the front, but even when we had gone over halfway through the letters the vast majority of students were still sitting down. Then I called out "N," and most of the students stood up – the letter 'N' represented the Phylum Arthropoda which makes up around 90 percent of all animals.

The effect was dramatic as 120+ students simultaneously came down to the front. This phylum exercise was certainly a dramatic one and a good example of a "context creation" activity.

CHAPTER 10
IMPROVING THE LECTURE

In a previous chapter we said that the lecture is so ingrained in higher education that over 95 percent of science professors in the nation use it Bligh (2000), despite the fact that there are calls to move towards implementing alternative instructional strategies that more actively involve students in their own learning (e.g., Chickering and Gamson, 1987). Does this mean that we should all abandon the lecture as an outdated and archaic teaching method? No. While the lecture has been criticized for its lack of effectiveness as an instructional strategy (Bland et al., 2007), it has been suggested that at least part of the reason that it has received such negative attention has more to do with teachers using it so poorly, than with its potential effectiveness as an instructional strategy (Kozma et al., 1978). So how can we use the lecture in a more effective manner?

 According to Bland et al. (2007), "McKeachie and Svinicki (2006) note that lectures are good because they:

a) are appropriate for communicating up-to-date information on the most current research and ideas related to the topics they are studying;

b) can summarize related information from scattered sources in a much more efficient way than if students were to read the sources on their own;

c) can be tailored to the specific interests of their audiences;

d) can enhance students' abilities to read relevant text; and can motivate students to learn more about the topic, particularly if the lecturer shows enthusiasm for the topic."

On the other hand Kozma et al., (1978) give the disadvantages of lectures as:

a)   essentially are a one-way mode of communication, giving the student little or no control over the nature, rate and flow of information. If used too much, this tends to promote intellectual passivity;

b)   prevent students from really experiencing the subject; and

c)   promote poor retention, a problem that is especially pronounced during longer lectures.

So a question to ask as you plan for each of your class meetings must be this one: "Is a lecture the best way for my students to achieve the desired outcomes?" If not, what would be a better way? If the material to be covered is content, lecture is the best format; if however, you are trying to develop problem-solving skills, analytical skills etc., then the lecture format is not appropriate.

If the lecture as the appropriate instructional strategy to employ, how do we use it effectively? According to Bland et al. (2007), "The central element in making lectures work is to *engage* students." But how do we engage students in content-heavy science courses?

Bland et al. (2007) suggest a number of different strategies. One major strategy we have already discussed is students' attention spans. As noted earlier, student attention span drops off as the class progresses. As a result, Hartley and Davies (1978) found that students recalled 70 percent of material presented in the first ten minutes of class, but only 20 percent presented in the last ten minutes.

Bland et al. (2007) also recommend that, "Variations in the pitch of one's voice, shifts in the intensity and pace of presentation, and even facial expression and movement about the classroom or lecture hall are often relatively easy for a lecturer to accommodate.....simply being more animated during a lecture can help."

Liven It Up—Humor

Humor is an additional effective strategy, as studies from the last 20 years suggest. Humor can reduce anxiety, decrease stress, and increase self-motivation. It can also enhance student learning, as Garner (2006) found that students showed an increase in retention of course content when exposed to lectures containing course-specific humor, as compared to those receiving the same course content without humor.

I use cartoons frequently in my classes. Remember to use cartoons/anecdotes which are related to the content of the lecture. In one of my courses that met on late Friday afternoons, I would end for the week by showing a number of cartoons, and students looked forward to them eagerly. However, keep in mind that you are not being paid to be a stand-up comic!

Another suggestion from Bland et al. (2007) is for lecturers to slow down. During lectures, instructors typically speak at rates between 120 to 240 words a minute, but it turns out that most students can write notes at an average rate of 20 words a minute. It is perhaps not surprising that Russell et al. (1984) found that medical students learned more in low-density lectures. Unfortunately the use of presentation software (i.e., PowerPoint etc.) tends to promote even faster delivery of notes, making it increasingly difficult for students to keep up.

 Randall (2000) promotes the "old-fashioned" way of teaching, using chalk!

".... Chalk enjoys the advantage of being slow: it takes time to write with it, and you need to get up and go to the blackboard to use it. . . chalk, hopelessly old-fashioned, by its very inefficiency helps to slow down the information flow and allows learning to take place."

Perhaps we should all try to teach a whole class with just chalk and the chalkboard and ask the students which produced the better learning. Of course chalk produces dust, and computer technology doesn't, but then chalk tends not to break down as often as technology!

Many instructors now routinely post lecture notes on the Web. Unfortunately, this encourages passivity and poor class attendance (Gray and Madson, 2007) – "why 'waste' time sitting through a lecture when all the notes are provided?" McKeachie & Svinicki (2006) suggests instructors provide an overall framework that the students can fill in by listening.

Gray and Madson (2007) suggest that you leave your notes partially incomplete by including:

- an organizational framework for the students to fill out,

- the labeled axes of graphs (leave the plotting to the students),

- diagrams (leave the labeling to the students),

- a table of data, omitting certain crucial figures,

- partially completed calculations, and

- a series of questions the students should be able to answer by the end of the lecture.

Gray and Madson (2007) recommend assigning one-minute papers—in-class assignments in which the teacher asks students to write for one-minute, usually about the main point(s) of the lecture, or the student's biggest question. Such papers, for obvious reasons, are usually assigned toward the end of the class period. The most typical topics include:

- What was the most important thing you learned during this class?

- What important question remains unanswered?

- What was the muddiest point?

The daily use of the one-minute paper has been found to increase student knowledge significantly (Chizmar and Ostrosky, 1998). While the one-minute paper has been shown to be quite effective it does require the instructor to collect and read the submissions, which obviously takes time, and unless one assigns some marks to the exercise students may not be prepared to put time and effort into it.

These authors also suggest that since students' frequency of studying is related to the frequency of accountability (ie., tests) there should be more frequent testing, such as daily quizzing. Such a quiz can be one short-answer or multiple-choice problem. While a good idea in principle, like the one-minute paper, it requires the instructor, or maybe a TA, to mark the quiz. Another option is to have students mark each other's quizzes but then it would be difficult to assign marks to answers in this way. Perhaps a better option is to pose a question and get students to respond using electronic clickers or colored response cards.

I close this chapter with a list of techniques for improving lectures that I use in my teaching workshops.

Twenty Techniques for Improving Lectures

1. Involve all class by maintaining eye contact.

2. Try to move away from lectern.

3. Be enthusiastic

4. Go over last time's material.

5. Use advanced organizers.

6. Display a guide to the lecture and refer to it.

7. Cover important/difficult parts while leaving easier material for students to learn on their own.

8. Read out notices etc. at the end of a lecture.

9. After 12-14 minutes change instructional style, or employ two-minute pauses.

10. Intersperse lecture with questions for students to answer.

11. Use both text and graphics for reinforcement.

12. Use concrete examples.

13. Distribute skeleton notes or partial notes for students to complete.

14. Relate material to students' interests, surroundings, etc.

15. Use humor, and especially cartoons, related to the material.

16. Summarize main points at end of lecture and look ahead to next period's material.

17. End class with journals, short writing assignments, concept maps, etc.

18. Encourage questions with written questions in box, exit slips, etc.

19. Use student representatives to give regular feedback.

20. Use a Web forum for posting notices, discussion of topics, raising questions out of class, etc.

CHAPTER 11
EVALUATION AND TESTING

Few science instructors have published papers about student evaluation in peer reviewed journals. When we deal with evaluation we must first ask, "What are the purposes of evaluation?" When we evaluate a student, we need to know why we are using a particular type of measure. The truth of the matter, I suspect, is that most instructors are not fully clear as to what they expect of students. This leads to students questioning scores they receive, suggesting that there is a difference between what instructors expect of their students, and what students think that their instructor expects of them.

Learning Objectives

Every course must have stated aims and objectives that clearly indicate what is expected of students, and how the students are expected to show that they have attained those objectives.

 An objective that states that students should learn everything they have been taught in a course is definitely not explicit enough, and doesn't define how the student demonstrates that they have learned everything.

Several decades ago Mager (1984) showed how course objectives could be written to indicate exactly how students were to be asked to demonstrate their knowledge. These "behavioral" objectives would clearly indicate to students what they needed to know, and how they would be expected to demonstrate that knowledge. An objective worded thusly: "To know the parts of an animal cell" is much too broad. A more specific behavioral objective is this: "Given an electronic micrograph of a typical animal cell a student will be expected to identify the following organelles – centriole, Golgi body, lysosome, mitochrondrion, rough EPR, ribosome." This objective only gives more detail about exactly what the student needs to know, but tells him/her how they will be expected to show that they have attained the requisite knowledge.

The behavioral objectives, if used, will cover the course content, but in addition it's important to specify the types of learning activities, or behaviors, expected of students. Do we want our students to simply "know" about the content, or be able to apply that knowledge in some other way, such as, for instance, to use that information to solve an unfamiliar problem?

Bloom's Toxonomy

In 1956, Bloom et. al. proposed a hierarchy of the various types of cognitive behaviors that educators might expect from their students. This taxonomy of educational objectives is still widely accepted today. This taxonomy distinguishes between six different levels of learning behaviors: (in ascending order) knowledge, comprehension, application, analysis, synthesis and evaluation. A brief summary of each level appears below together with an example.

KNOWLEDGE

1. **Knowledge** (*recall of information*).

   example: To list the phases of animal cell division.

INTELLECTUAL ABILITIES AND SKILLS

2. **Comprehension** (*type of understanding in which the individual knows what is being communicated and can make use of the material*).

   example: Being able to solve an equation.

3. **Application** (*the use of abstractions*).

    example: Being able to predict the probable effects of a change in the numbers of producers, herbivores, or carnivores in a named food web.

4. **Analysis** (*the breakdown of a communication into its constituent elements such that the hierarchy of ideas is made clear and/or the relationships between the ideas are made explicit*).

    example: Being able to read a passage about an experiment and to identify the problem under investigation, the researcher's hypothesis, methodology, results and conclusions, as well as the control and experimental set-ups.

5. **Synthesis** (*putting together the elements and parts so as to form a whole*).

    example: Being able to write a scientific essay using an excellent organization of ideas and statements.

6. **Evaluation** (*making judgements about the value of materials and methods for given purposes*).

    example: Being able to critically evaluate a scientific report and comment on the appropriateness of the procedures used, the accuracy of statistical analyses, and the conclusions derived.

While this abbreviated description gives only a brief review of Bloom et. al.'s taxonomy of educational objectives, it should make it clear that tests and assignments given to students should evaluate their progress towards the course objectives. Test items should be of sufficient variety to test the different levels of understanding. Multiple-choice items, fill-in-the blank items, and questions asking for named examples tend to test the lower levels of the hierarchy, particularly "knowledge," while essay questions usually test the higher-level "synthesis" skill. The highest level skill in the taxonomy, "evaluation," is not a type of skill which lends itself to inclusion in most test situations.

Assignments

Assignments can come in all shapes and forms including tests, written assignments, laboratory reports, final examinations, and even oral presentations and examinations. All assignments should cover course objectives. I will concentrate here on tests and examinations. In most science courses these account for the bulk of grades given in a course.

Types of Tests and Examinations

I find test-grids useful in the development of tests.

"Test grids have been used for decades to facilitate the planning of tests and examinations, as instruments to classify existing test items, and to analyze existing examinations for content and the intellectual skills demanded (cognitive demand). Such grids are usually two-dimensional with content areas comprising one dimension, and intellectual skills or taxonomic levels, the other..." (Jungwirth 1992).

When constructing major examinations that cover a variety of different content areas, it is also important to ensure that there is a reasonable correlation between the number of items, the percentage of the grade they represent, and the amount of class time spent on them during the semester.

Multiple-Choice

Clearly a variety of types of questions should be used on tests and examinations to adequately test the different cognitive levels of understanding. Multiple-choice tests are becoming increasingly popular with many science instructors since the answers to such questions are easy to score when using marking templates or computerized scanning. Unfortunately, however, such multiple-choice questions tend to test at the lower levels of Bloom et al.'s (1956) taxonomy. Nowadays many textbooks come with access to multiple-choice test items. I have to admit a personal bias against multiple-choice tests, and use them very rarely.

True/False Items

True/false items are not often used at the college/university level since there is a 50 percent chance that a student can guess the correct answer.

Problems

Problem-type questions can include a wide variety of different types of problem solving exercises. In order to test students at the higher levels of Bloom's taxonomy, I always include a number of problems on tests. The problem could be a genetics problem, interpreting diagrams, graphs or tables of data, or an account of an experiment with students asked to identify poor procedures and conclusions together with suggestions for improvements. I include some examples in the appendix as possible models for your own questions. Problem-solving questions are particularly useful in Chemistry and Physics examinations.

Essay Questions

Essay questions are probably the easiest to develop but the toughest to grade because of the variability in student responses. These kinds of questions are useful for evaluating the higher levels of Bloom's taxonomy—particularly analysis and synthesis. However, they are not so useful at covering large amounts of course content. When class sizes are relatively small, always include one or more essay questions. Essay style questions should probably not be used if you have TA's helping you grade tests due to the variability in marking that may result. One option, however, is to grade the essay questions on all the student tests, then leave the TA's to grade the objective questions.

Open Book Examinations

With this type of testing students are allowed to bring class notes, and even textbooks into the examination. While students tend to like the idea of having their own notes and the text to refer to during the examination, instructors tend to regard this type of examination as making things too easy for the students. In my own experience, however, I have found that such examination formats tend to favour the well-prepared students who do not have to rely on continuous reference to their notes and other aids. Students who depend too much on such aids spend too much time going through their notes and texts, and end up not having enough time answering the questions! A major advantage of this type of examination, however, is that it significantly reduces the likelihood of cheating as students have open access to their own notes and texts.

Take-Home Examinations

Take-home examinations can be particularly useful in upper undergraduate courses where the instructor requires the students to carry out background research and incorporate research literature in their responses. Such examinations are usually given out a few days ahead of the submission deadline. I routinely use this style of examination with a senior level science education class. While there is the possibility of student collusion on answers, if the classes are small it is relatively easy for the instructor to detect such cheating. Students tend to dislike this form of examination as it can require a lot of background work and so can be very time-consuming.

Oral Examinations

With small classes it might also be possible to employ oral examinations. Hartman (1995) describes such an experiment and concluded that: "Our experiences have convinced us that the oral examination is an excellent and immediate teaching tool, which helps propel the learning process forward. It is rewarding and empowering for the student to recognize that once she gets beyond a particular point of confusion or a forgotten fact she is able to participate in a discourse, and use her knowledge in new combinations and explanations."

However, Hartman also says that oral examinations are practical in classes of up to only twelve students as they are time intensive.

Testing Tips

One problem associated with the development of tests in the sciences is "ringing the changes," that is, having a number of alternative forms of test items. No matter how good a test is the first time, it doesn't take long for the questions, and, more importantly, the answers, to become widely circulated among students. I remember one occasion reading a large number of similar, but incorrect, responses to one particular question. Then the explanation suddenly occurred to me – this question was an adaptation of one I had used several times before, but with a different answer this time around. The responses I was reading were the correct ones for the previously worded question!

Hartman (1995) and Orzechowski (1995), among others, have suggested the idea of having students themselves construct possible test items.

A common problem with administering tests, especially in large classes, is what to do with student who miss a test. Do you give them the same test that you used with the rest of the class, produce an alternative for them or what? Geske (1992) recommends giving four in-class tests and a final examination, and requiring that students must complete four of the five. Therefore, if a student misses a test, it is not necessary to produce a make-up exam. This is a technique I have used since I first came across it, and it has saved me a lot of time and trouble, particularly in large classes.

Another issue which always arises is students coming to you and saying that their tests have been incorrectly graded. In an attempt to overcome this problem and at the same time use the test as a teaching tool, Martin (1985) has come up with an innovative approach. After an examination she initially only returns the question pages and the students form into groups to come up with the correct responses. This search for possible answers can involve textbooks, notes, laboratory equipment etc., but cannot include asking the instructor. When all the groups are finished, the instructor calls out the number of each question and asks for group answers. When groups disagree on a particular answer, they can resolve their own differences by arguing or stating their preferences. The students individually record the correct answers. Upon completion of this exercise the actual graded answer sheets are returned. According to Martin (1985), "The students no longer complain of ambiguous or "tricky" questions. Instead, they focus on themselves, trying to discover why some answers are incorrect."

 A strategy that I have used is to return graded papers with no comments written on them. I tell the students to go over their papers to see if they can correct their mistakes.

Of course computers can be used to not only eliminate the drudgery of grading, but can provide instantaneous feedback to students, and can also provide immediate feedback to the instructor as to how the class as a whole is performing. The statistics from such tests can be used to identify poorly answered items and then re-teach the material causing the problem. Earlier studies (e.g., Collins and Fletcher, 1985) showed that this type of "remedial" teaching can lead to impressive increases in student scores on later in-class written tests. Though I don't advocate a heavy reliance on computer-administered testing, such tests can be particularly useful as weekly tests, with or without grades being allotted to them. Such tests can provide feedback to students on their progress, and allow instructors to quickly identify students with weaknesses, and to identify topics in need of remedial teaching. Optional tests placed on the class web page allow students to self-test themselves on a regular basis.

Evaluation is very much a matter of personal preference, and so different instructors will differ in their choice of evaluation methods. In multi-section courses, many of the examinations may be common to all sections and so an individual instructor may have little input into the development of such tests. If you are new to science teaching, obtain as many past copies of tests and examinations as possible for the course(s) you will be teaching. Use them as models for your own tests until you are more experienced with test development.

When you give a test, make notes of changes you would like to make, including the correction of errors, replacing misleading diagrams, re-writing poor questions and the like. Keep these notes together with a copy of the actual examination.

Remember that there is no such thing as a perfect test or examination, and even after teaching the same course for twenty years, I am still perfecting the tests that I give.

Grade Review Policy

In large classes particularly, another problem which arises is that a number of students will inevitably complain that their papers have been incorrectly graded, and ask you to re-mark them. In response, I developed a Grade Review Policy (Figure 11.1) statement that clearly indicates when and how I will re-mark tests. By using such policy statements, you can reduce the number of students asking for exams and papers to be re-marked.

Figure 11.1 Grade Review Policy

BIOLOGY 2040

GRADE REVIEW POLICY

If you are of the opinion that your paper has been incorrectly marked, you may appeal the marking by following the underlying procedures.

1. If the problem is a mathematical error in adding up marks, indicate this problem at the top of the front page and hand in your paper to have the mark adjusted.

2. If the problem is a disagreement with the mark(s) assigned to one or more answers, document on a separate sheet of paper why you think that your answer(s) is worth more marks by reference to the marking scheme. You should refer to class notes, textbook etc. as and when appropriate.

NOTE: I will not accept as valid reasons for re-grading an assignments comments such as:

"My friend received a higher grade for the same answer."

"It deserves a higher grade."

While every effort is taken to ensure that all assignments are graded in the same way, there will inevitably be some discrepancies. Papers that are to be re-graded should be handed in no later than two weeks after the papers are returned. *Papers will not be re-graded after that date.*

Another important (though often neglected) testing tool is the office hour. Offer optional class meetings in anticipation of a major test or examination. Tell students that these meetings are not revision periods, but rather that you will be there to answer any questions that they have. Keep in mind that students are sometimes not confident enough to ask questions in front of their classmates. Allow questions to be submitted in a variety of ways: in advance of the class (by e-mail, class web forum, or dropping them off at my office prior to the class). Encourage students to leave written questions on your desk at the start of the period. Not only do such sessions allow students to have their questions answered, but it also allows the instructor to get a fairly good feel for the class's understanding of topics.

Another tool I have used to assist students who seem to consistently perform poorly on tests is to give them a key to help them identify the source(s) of their problems. For each incorrect response on a test, the student works through the key which ends up giving them advice related to their particular difficulty.

CHAPTER 12
WRITING AND WRITTEN ASSIGNMENTS

In recent years there has been a virtual explosion of interest in the whole area of writing as it applies to science students, and as part of the Writing Across the Curriculum (WAC for short) movement many science instructors require students to write more than ever before. Unfortunately, this WAC movement comes at a time when colleges and universities, coping with the pressure of educating larger numbers of students without an increase in the necessary resources, have moved to larger classes, particularly at the introductory levels. This move to larger classes has made it even more difficult to assign and grade written assignments. Given these realities dare I recommend that all science students do more writing at a time when harried instructors are struggling just to keep afloat? Absolutely!

The skill of writing is an important one for *all* students irrespective of their chosen profession. In science, writing is the main method by which we communicate the results of our research. Unfortunately, science instructors often do not teach their students how to write papers and laboratory reports because they assume that students learn enough about writing in their English classes (Hotchkiss and Nellis, 1988). Science writing, however, is a different form of writing from those in many other disciplines. Tobias (1989), a sociologist by training, has examined writing as it applies to the sciences and she says: "I have long been aware of the contrast between a scientist's view of writing and my own. Clear, precise statements, closely reasoned arguments, unambiguous and very often felicitous use of language are much admired and sought after among scientists."

There is then a significant difference between the writing a science instructor expects of his or her students, and the style of writing taught in English classes.

Science instructors must realize that it is an important part of their jobs to teach students the techniques of science writing.

Of course in addition to the actual process of writing, "We also want students to become familiar with conducting searches of scientific literature to find journal and review articles pertaining to the scientific investigation about which they are writing" (Jacobson and Wilson, 1991).

In addition, therefore, to the actual process of writing we also need to address the issue of teaching students the necessary research skills—including on-line searches. Your college/university library will probably offer such programs, either general in nature, or tailored to your specific requirements. If you do intend to have your students produce written assignments incorporating literature searches, consult with your institution's library staff first.

While most of us are convinced of the importance of our students writing, it is no easy thing to do in large introductory science classes. When I was faced a few years ago with increasing class size I had decided that assigning written work to my students was no longer practical given the time it took to mark such assignments. Around that same time I attended a science education conference where one of the presenters gave a talk on a powerful reason for students writing frequently – it actually improves their understanding of the subject matter, and, therefore, their grades in science courses.

Writing as a Way of Learning

Randy Moore has spent many years investigating the role of writing in biology, and has taught a course entitled "Writing to learn Biology." Some of the tenets on which this course is based include:

"Writing is one of the most powerful tools for discovering, organizing, and communicating knowledge. Many of our thoughts only exist when put on paper....writing is a powerful tool for learning because it helps you to discover, develop, and organize your ideas. Poor writing often indicates poor understanding or faulty science" (Moore, 1994).

The basic tenets of writing to learn, therefore, can be summarized as – students learn as they write; ideas form as the pen hits the page; and writing creates meaning. These tenets sound quite reasonable, but is there any hard evidence that writing about science improves learning of science? The answer is a definitive yes as Moore's (1994) work, among others, has demonstrated. What follows are some ideas as to how to integrate writing assignments in science courses.

Short Writing Assignments

A number of years ago I used to set a compulsory written assignment worth 20 percent for the students in one of my courses. They could write it on a topic of their choice related to the course content. It was not unusual to receive papers in excess of 50 pages, often handwritten. I can still remember reading (plowing?) through these assignments. At the time, I was writing a monthly column for a local newspaper and I had been told that in future my columns would be reduced from 1,500 words, in total, to just 1,000.

The next semester, therefore, I imposed a strict one thousand word limit on the assignment—approximately four pages of double-spaced typewriting. My students were delighted to hear that they only had to write a one-thousand word assignment. The general sentiment seemed to be that it would be too easy! However, it didn't take them long to realize that it was much more difficult than writing a very long assignment.

From my point of view it was so much easier to grade these shorter assignments. Marking these assignments became even easier when I started to use an instrument called an assignment attachment which I will discuss later on.

Annotated Abstracts

Foos (1987) has described another short piece of writing called the 'annotated abstract' which he suggests "works not only to enhance students' writing skills, but it also improves their thinking skills." Before the students write an annotated abstract they must read, comprehend, interpret, and analyze an article from a scientific journal. Foos writes that "in a single assignment, the instructor can introduce students to scientific journals, include a reading assignment, and provide an opportunity for students to practice writing."

The annotated abstract has three main parts: the citation, the abstract, and an analysis, or critique, of the article. Foos recommends weekly abstracts over a six to ten week period during the semester, and suggests limiting the assignment to a double-spaced page. The abstracts can be scored out of 5 with half-points deducted for each error, whether grammatical, punctuational, spelling, or confounding the point of the article. Foos gives four benefits for assigning such an assignment:

- First, writing abstracts helps the students develop their writing skills.

- Second, in preparing abstracts, the students are obliged to read articles from the professional literature they would otherwise have missed.

- Third, the student must think about the information they have read and analyze it in the context of what they have learned.

- Finally, assigning abstracts helps the students develop confidence in themselves.

Microthemes

Recent evidence from a wide variety of disciplines, including mathematics and science, has shown that students who write frequently about their subject learn the subject better than those who don't. So how do we get our students to write frequently? One possibility is using very short pieces of writing called microthemes. Microthemes were first developed by James Work (1979) for a literature course, and were later extended to a number of other disciplines.

"Microthemes are a special kind of student writing whose length is strictly limited, usually to 150 to 400 words" (Leahy 1994).

Microthemes are graded for their ideas rather than for grammar and spelling. The short length of a microtheme allows for quick marking. I have used microthemes in a large (approximately 200) second-year non-majors course for a number of years. Students can elect either to write a one-thousand word assignment, or complete weekly microthemes. Below are some examples of the microthemes I have used:

- "Food additives are not natural constituents of food and should not therefore be added to foods. Discuss this statement."

- "In the 1980's it was assumed that we would soon be able to eliminate infectious diseases altogether. Now in the 1990s we realize that this may never happen. Explain."

- "A friend suffering from influenza visits the doctor and is given a prescription for antibiotics. Would you advise your friend to obtain and use the antibiotics? Explain your answer."

An analysis of four years worth of data from this course shows that students writing the microthemes performed better on tests and examinations than those not using them. The analysis also showed that the greater the number of microthemes a student completes the better the performance on tests and examinations (Collins, 2004).

Not only then do microthemes contribute to better student learning, but common errors that surface in microthemes enable the instructor to go over the misunderstood material in class so that all students, including those not writing microthemes, can benefit.

Journal Writing

The technique of having students keep journals for their courses is becoming increasingly common in a number of disciplines at the college/university level, including the sciences. The student records both information and a personal reaction to this information. Journal keeping is meant to actively engage the students in the course content. Trombulak and Sheldon (1989) have demonstrated that something as simple as optional, non-graded, journal writing can significantly improve learning in biology, a finding that has, of course, been demonstrated for other forms of writing.

While Trombulak and Sheldon (1989) did not require students to write journals and did not check them, others such as Cannon (1990) do read and grade the student journals. Cannon requires a minimum of three entries per week, and collects the journals about every two weeks.

"Since I consider this to be 'free' writing, I don't worry much about style. I do like to see a modicum of punctuation and a bit of paragraph development, but what I am really looking for is the sense that they are exploring the discipline through free writing."

Cannon (1990) grades each journal with "a check," "check-plus," or "check-minus" depending on their efforts. While Cannon (1990) and Trombulak and Sheldon (1989) have their students write up their journals outside of class, Ambron (1987) sets aside 5 minutes of each 50 minute class for students to write up their journals, and she collects and reads the student journals a few times each semester. She also keeps her own journal and writes that, "It has enabled me to examine my personal reactions to different classes and to evaluate certain methods of presentation."

An instructor's journal has the added benefit of contributing to a betterment in the instructor's own style of teaching, something that all of us should be doing.

Assignment Attachment

An assignment attachment is a useful device to assist in both grading written assignments and providing useful feedback to students on their assignments. Since adopting the assignment attachment, not only is grading an assignment much easier, but fewer students request re-reads as the attachment gives a very good indication of where they did not do too well, and how they could improve their writing. Students find feedback useful, and many will keep the attachment and use it in other courses which require a writing assignment since it provides information on aspects in which they could improve their writing.

Posters

While posters are not strictly speaking, written assignments, they do include writing and are of course, a different type of assignment which can be given to classes in place of term papers and the like. Posters are usually group projects so you will have to decide as to whether each member of the group will receive the same mark for the poster, or, if not, how you intend to allocate marks to the individual members of a group. Evaluating posters can include a variety of 'presentation' options. If time permits each group could be asked to make a verbal presentation to the class on their poster, and marks could be assigned to this presentation, as well as to the actual poster. If time does not permit this the alternatives are either, to set aside a time in class, or at some other time, for the posters to be displayed for the whole class to view, and class members to ask questions of the groups responsible for the posters. You should also view and judge each poster, but also ask the group questions about it with the quality of their answers also contributing to the noted marks for each poster.

Portfolios

A portfolio is defined as, "A purposeful collection of student work that tells the story of the students' efforts, progress, or achievement in (a) given area" (Arter and Spandel, 1992).

A portfolio contains a variety of different types of work. It might include, for instance, a piece of writing on the topic by the student, copies of articles relating to the topic together with brief summaries, photos, drawings, brief summaries of television programs the student has viewed, and even audiotapes etc., of interviews with experts in that subject area. However, the portfolio is not just a random assortment of materials, but must also be catalogued and there should be a written summary explaining why each item was placed in the portfolio.

CHAPTER 13
LABORATORY SESSIONS AND FIELD TRIPS

Laboratory Sessions

In recent years there has been a disturbing trend in which many universities have dropped the laboratory component altogether from their large introductory science courses. Increasing enrollments, insufficient numbers of teaching assistants, costs of equipment and materials, and the enormous time burden on instructors have all been cited as reasons for dropping the laboratory component. Why, then, are laboratories so important and how can we make the most of them at a time when there is pressure to eliminate them altogether?

(Wilson and Stensvold, 1991) have summarized the goals of laboratory instruction as the following.

Through their participation in laboratory experiences, students should:

1. Develop a practical capability of laboratory technique and methods, including safe working practices that are essential to obtaining reliable and accurate information.

2. Experience and learn about the universe firsthand, including the biological, physical and chemical viewpoints, and comprehending the materials and processes essential to each.

3. Comprehend, illustrate, explain and apply science concepts. Relate these concepts to theories and theoretical structures that explain them.

4. Apply facts and principles to new and novel situations, including 'real world concerns', using appropriate analytical, creative, and critical thinking skills.

5. Promote scientific thinking and methodology, accepting new ideas but demanding testability with appropriate analysis as a basis for making reasoned judgements and decisions."

In an earlier survey (Sundberg and Armstrong, 1993) found that, "At most institutions, laboratory instruction involves a combination of modified versions of commercial laboratory manual exercises, exercises obtained at workshops or conferences, and exercises developed internally."

While there is interest in investigative types of laboratories as a method of teaching students science by allowing them to do science, (Sundberg and Armstrong, 1993) conclude that this approach, while especially successful at small liberal arts colleges, has been less widely employed at larger institutions. The tendency, then, has been to employ structured "recipe-type" laboratory exercises which are predictable and secure, but are often dull and tedious—little is left to the imagination (Tamir and Lunetta, 1981). Most undergraduate laboratory exercises then, are usually for learning laboratory techniques, carrying out recipe-type experiments, and reinforcing lecture material by examination of specimens, and the like. However, laboratory exercises can offer a number of things that lectures cannot.

- Students can learn to act as scientists by actually performing experiments, and learn firsthand about the various elements of the scientific method;

- Students get to handle laboratory equipment;

- Students learn the various types of laboratory skills required for higher-level courses;

- Students get to handle and work with live organisms and observe first-hand how they move, feed, breathe, excrete, reproduce. etc... activities which are not always possible to view in lectures;

- Laboratory sessions allow students to discuss science with each other, and to work cooperatively, activities which are more closely related to the ways in which scientists actually work;

- The hands on, interactive, nature of the laboratory setting helps students develop positive attitudes toward science.

In all probability, as part-time instructors you may have little input into the laboratories designed for the course(s) you will teach, but it is always useful to see if some of the usual recipe-type laboratory exercises could be replaced by more inquiry-type exercises.

In biology, for example, students are often expected to conduct transpiration experiments and to observe leaf cross sections under the microscope. Rather than just view a number of different leaf cross sections under the microscope and be told that they are from desert, aquatic or terrestrial plants, an alternative is for students to observe a typical leaf and then be asked to decide on which environments other plants (leaf cross sections) come from, and explain why. This simple adaptation allows students to discuss options with each other and to undertake genuine investigatory science.

Computers and Laboratories

Nowadays, computers can be used for a variety of purposes in undergraduate science laboratories—especially for data collection and analysis, and for running simulations.

Data Acquisition

Computers facilitate the collection of large amounts of data in a relatively short time period, and allow students more time to investigate the effects of various experimental parameters. A wide variety of computer interfaces have been developed for use in teaching laboratories. These include temperature probes, pH meters, and a whole series of interfaces for physiological experiments, such as reaction time to various stimuli. Leonard (1988) lists the following benefits to student learning, of using computer interfaces to laboratory instruments in biology. Obviously, the benefits apply to other sciences as well:

1. Interfacing is cost effective.

2. Interfacing can save student time and boredom since the students are freed from repetitive data recording tasks, giving them more time for more productive and challenging activities.

3. Learning to use the instrumentation of modern technology is fun and motivating to students, since they enjoy using current technology and appreciate the opportunity of learning to use instruments that might be useful outside school.

4. Interfacing can make data analysis much simpler and conceptually more meaningful since most interfacing apparatus allows the students to instantaneously see a graph on the screen that illustrates the relationship between independent and dependent variables.

5. Students can effectively learn science concepts and skills using interfacing.

6. Using microcomputer interfacing may allow students who are not formal thinkers to bridge the gap between concrete and formal thought so they can understand abstract science concepts. Since students can see on the screen a concrete result of manipulating variables, they may be more likely to understand the abstract relationship between those variables than by collecting and analyzing data in the traditional, manual fashion.

7. Greater opportunities for creativity, problem solving, and the development of reasoning skills are likely indirect consequences of the direct benefits of using computer interfacing.

Computer interfacing then is a technology with great potential in undergraduate science laboratories and students should continually be exposed to it before they graduate and work in environments where such technology is taken for granted.

Simulations

A major use of computers in science laboratories is in the running of simulations, but just when should one use a simulation rather than perform the actual experiment? Steed (1992) suggests, "Simulations are desirable when: performing experiments would be impossible, the experiment would be too dangerous, or the time frame to perform experiments is too long. A simulation allows control of one parameter at a time, that might not be possible to do in the real world."

With all the discussion nowadays about animal rights, a number of dissection simulations have been developed, so that one might add another reason for performing simulations to Steed's (1992) list: that of using simulations when ethical issues may argue against performing real experiments or learning certain skills.

 There is certainly a place for computer simulations in undergraduate science laboratories provided that one takes heed: Undergraduate laboratory exercises shouldn't just become simulations since they are faster to complete, and less expensive because they don't use costly chemicals, biological specimens and expensive equipment.

Unfortunately, for many students, laboratories are just boring, repetitive periods which do not allow them to experience the excitement of science. I suspect many undergraduate science laboratories turn off many students to a career in science when they should be doing quite the opposite. It's crucial, then, to make laboratory sessions much more interesting, hands-on, and exciting so that students experience science in a way they cannot in lectures.

Field Trips

While most scientists, and particularly biologists, environmental scientists, and earth scientists/geologists, would agree that practical field experiences are important components of a student's undergraduate education, the reality is that fewer students are having such experiences during their undergraduate careers. In a study conducted for the Association of American Colleges and the American Institute of Biological Sciences, Carter et. al. (1990) found that somewhere between 20 and 25 percent of biology majors had never completed a field course, and that field courses for non-majors were practically non-existent.

Faculty also reported a decline to near demise, of field experiences in the undergraduate biology curriculum. At a time of increasing environmental problems, fewer and fewer students are actually involved in studies of the natural environment at first-hand.

Field trips and field studies are important, but there is pressure on us as instructors to decrease, or even eradicate field experiences for our students. How are we to defend the position that such field experiences are necessary parts of a student's education? Carter (1993) suggests that:

"Our failure to expose all citizens, including those with a secondary education as well as those with advanced degrees outside the sciences, to the natural sciences through participating field study, has resulted in a world inundated by a single species that is incapable of making those basic decisions vital to the future of the planet. We are asking the world's human population to make long term decisions that require considerable knowledge of such basic concepts as evolution and ecology without ever providing science education in the appropriate environment."

It is only by experiencing the natural environment that we can appreciate the interplay of organisms and their environment, and the factors which can lead to an alteration of the natural balance. It has been my personal observation that people only come to appreciate and protect their natural environment after they have come to experience it themselves and have learnt about its resident animals and plants. Such experience of the natural environment, ". . .cannot be replaced by a classroom or laboratory experience, a computer program or a lecture" Carter (1993).

Besides the actual hands-on experience that students gain while on field trips there are other tangible outcomes, and such trips promote active learning, encourage student collaboration, and ensure the relevance of higher education instruction Beiesdorfer and Davis (1994). Orien and Hofstein (1991) report that student attitudes to field instruction reflect at least five dimensions which can be viewed as positive goals or outcomes of field instruction. These five are:

- Disciplinary learning

- Individualized learning

- A social aspect

- An adventure aspect

- An environmental consciousness aspect

The social exchange resulting from increased instructor-student interaction may contribute to positive affective development (Schwab and Brandwein 1962). There are many good and sound reasons for including field trips and field courses in both the programs of science majors and non-majors.

Clearly the expenses of such field courses and field trips are major contributing factors in the general reduction in such outdoor ventures but another significant factor, perhaps, relates to the instructors themselves, as Beiesdorfer and Davis (1994) note: "Perhaps the reason more instructors do not include field trips in their courses is because trips require a great amount of pre-planning and have a great potential for disaster."

I suspect that another reason why instructors are not overly keen on conducting field trips and courses is their own lack of knowledge of the environment. This is, of course, a real Catch 22 situation, for if today's instructors do not conduct field courses and field trips, then their students will not learn about the local natural environment, and they, in turn as instructors will probably be even less likely to conduct field courses and field trips for their students.

If the cost of transportation and the time involved in the transporting of students to remote sites are drawbacks, select sites on campus, or within easy walking distance. In recent years, I have conducted mini-field trips around the campus, or walks to a nearby river to investigate such things as the effect of pollution on aquatic invertebrates.

Even if the course you are teaching does not include provisions for field trips, etc., or provide a budget in support of field trips, this should not mean that you need to abandon the idea. There are a variety of different exercises that can be carried out in the campus grounds.

One particular type of activity is the one-metre square field trip. Different groups are assigned to different types of environment such as garden, lawn, footpath, under coniferous/deciduous trees etc..., and each group randomly chooses a one meter-square area in that particular environment. The exercise could be a botanical one to document all the plants in the square, or to calculate the area covered by each type of plant, or zoological ones to list all the animals found in that area.

In addition to field courses and field trips as out-of-classroom learning activities, there are also what may be termed site visits to specific centers such as aquaria, zoological gardens, wildlife parks, botanical gardens, museums, geological centers, and science centers. Many of these centers have their own educational staff and offer organized tours for educational groups. Often such tours can be tailored to meet the visiting instructor's objectives.

Many universities and colleges offer field courses at freshwater, marine and terrestrial field centers which are also open to students at other universities, with the latter awarding transfer credit to the student upon successful completion of the course. There are also a number of private organizations that run field courses throughout the year on a variety of subject areas, and for a wide range of educational levels. There are even courses offered on board ships cruising to exotic parts of the world (e.g., Arctic, Antarctic, Galapagos Islands, etc.). Even, therefore, if the institution at which you teach does not offer such outdoor experiences, it might be useful to advertise such opportunities available elsewhere to your students, so that they can benefit from an outdoor experience.

The opportunities then for field-based activities are immense, ranging from activities planned by the instructor out of doors on campus property to expensive, elaborate cruises and courses offered in other parts of the world. What matters most is not the type of activity experienced by students, but that all science undergraduates actually experience field-based activities for themselves.

Figure 13.1

CHAPTER 14
DEALING WITH MISCONCEPTIONS ABOUT SCIENCE

Misconceptions & Non-Science Majors

Though this in one of the shortest chapters in this handbook, it is also one of the most important, and the topic one of the most challenging for instructors and students alike.

The field of student misconceptions of science has been the subject of considerable research during the last few decades, and a number of international conferences have had this topic as their sole focus. When we teach science, it is useful to know the types of misconceptions students might have so that we can attempt to correct them before we teach new material which builds on previously learned material. Fisher et, al. (1986) in their studies of learning science suggest that, "Learning about an academic subject implies learning a specialized vocabulary, concepts and ideas, as well as learning the complex web of interrelationships between them."

Fisher et al. (1986) claim that during a lecture a student picks up a vague sense of a main idea along with half a dozen or so associated words (e.g., for protein synthesis the words would be DNA, mRNA, tRNA, ribosomes, translation, transcription, amino-acids and protein). However, the exact nature of the individual concepts, and the relationships between them are not generally clear to the students, nor are the details of the process.

Even though beginners may acquire vocabulary rapidly, it may take years of study and experience before they develop levels of meaning similar to experts in the field. Such findings explain why both majors and non-majors in introductory science courses seem to have no difficulty defining terms on examinations, but often encounter considerable difficulty answering questions asking for explanations of relationships between terms (i.e., explain and compare/contrast questions).

It is, then, not surprising that student knowledge of science contains all sorts of errors and misconceptions. But what exactly are misconceptions? Wandersee (1985) writes that "the term 'misconception' is often used to describe an unaccepted (though not necessarily 'incorrect') interpretation of a concept by the learner."

Here are some examples of common science student misconceptions:

- All plant cells possess chloroplasts;

- Individual organisms can evolve;

- Animals respire, but plants photosynthesize

As Doran (1972) writes, "If a teacher ascertains which misconceptions are prevalent among the entire class or a few members of the class, the teacher can guide students along an instructional sequence that may aid development of a more reasonable understanding of the phenomena or principles."

Clearly, it is not practical to try to test every student's understanding of a topic prior to its teaching to find out what misconceptions students may have. However, with a bit of time, one can usually identify many of the misconceptions held by students, and it is possible to alter one's teaching methods to take account of such common misconceptions:

Read examination essay question answers carefully. Keep in mind that it may be frustrating or disappointing to catalog all the examples of misinformation written by your students after you have taught them! However, it must be done. Student success and retention do, after all, rely on whether or not students master the material of a particular course.

Johnstone and Mahmoud (1980) in a study, not actually of misconceptions, but of topics of difficulty in biology, have devised a technique to identify topics of high perceived difficulty in biology syllabi. Even though it takes time to go through examinations to identify misconceptions and identify topics of difficulty, the reward is that you can take account of this information the next time you teach the same course.

Using Discrepant Events

Wright (1981) defines a discrepant event as "a phenomenon which occurs that seems to run contrary to our first line of reasoning."

Discrepant events can be good devices to stimulate interest in learning science concepts and principles. Such discrepant events can also be used to motivate and provoke active student participation (Wright and Govindarajan, 1992). The use of discrepant events in the classroom focuses students' attention, and challenges them to explain the event which seems to challenge the normal view of how events are meant to proceed.

A classic discrepant event is the sinking ice-cube trick. A normal ice cube (made of water) is added to what appears to be water, but the cube proceeds to sink to the bottom of the container. How come? Isn't ice meant to float? So what has happened here? Well what has happened is that the liquid in the container is not water, but alcohol, and since the ice cube has a higher density than alcohol, it sinks into the alcohol.

This, then, is a good example of a discrepant event, and there are numerous examples which can be used in chemistry and physics. Such discrepant events are not as commonly encountered in biology although Wright and Govindarajan have listed a number for Biology (1992). Wright and Govindarajan (1995) have published a book containing over 200 discrepant events to which you can refer.

CHAPTER 15
CLOSING COMMENTS

Earlier chapters of this book have introduced you to students and how they vary in their learning styles, and various types of teaching strategies which encourage active learning by your students. We have also looked at the importance of writing, not only as a method of communication but also as a way of learning. The use of technology in teaching has also been addressed in some detail, realizing of course that technology changes so rapidly that we need to keep abreast of newer technologies which hold out promise for use in the teaching/learning enterprise. In this final chapter I want to stress the importance of pedagogical societies, journals, and meetings.

Pedagogical Journals/Conferences etc....

Most of the ideas in this book were ones I first came across by reading educational journals and attending conferences and teaching workshops. If I hadn't read these journals or attended these meetings, I would not have become familiar with some very useful teaching strategies, and my teaching, and my students' learning, would not have been as successful!

I cannot stress how important reading pedagogical journals and attending conferences and workshops is! Not only do you learn about new approaches and ideas, but if you attend meetings you also get to meet other colleagues with whom you can keep in contact and with whom you can share ideas and information. As a part-time instructor you may not get the chance to travel to meetings, unless they occur locally, but your institution may offer teaching-related workshops you may be able to attend. Even if you can't attend meetings you should be able to read pedagogical journals appropriate to your discipline, a number of which will be in your department or in the institution's library.

Discipline-specific journals, as well as the *Journal of College Science Teaching* (JCST), are usually part of a membership to the relevant society. JCST, for example, is available through a subscription to the National Science Teachers Association (NSTA). NSTA also has an affiliate, the Society for College Science Teaching (SCST).

By and large, you can count on the discipline-specific periodicals to cover all teaching levels from secondary school through university.

Postscript

Well I think you have heard enough from me, so now it's time to get on with the teaching! I hope you have picked up a number of useful pointers in this book which you will employ in your teaching.

I wish you the best in your teaching career, and hope you have as enjoyable an experience as I have been fortunate to have in my career. Always remember why you are in the classroom – for the benefit of your students, and not yourself – and you should do well. What other profession allows you to continually associate with bright young minds and to influence so many young people? Always keep your students first in mind, and you won't go too far wrong!

References

Ambron, J. 1987. "Writing to improve learning in Biology." *Journal of College Science Teaching*, XVI, 4, 263-266.

Angelo, T.A. 1991. "Learning in the classroom (Phase I)". A report from the Lawrence Hall of Science, University of California at Berkeley, California.

Arter, J. and Spandel, V. 1992. NCME Instructional Module: Using portfolios of student work in instruction and assessment. Educational Measurement: Issues and Practice, 11(1), 36-44.

Atkinson, M., Wilson, T., and Kidd, J. 2008. "Virtual education: teaching and learning in Second Life." *Teaching and Learning in Higher Education*, 50:1.

Ault, C.A. 1985. "Concept mapping as a study strategy in Earth Science." *Journal of College Science Teaching*, 1, 38-45.

Barbe, W.B., and Milone, M.N. 1981. "What we know about modality strengths." *Educational Leadership*, February, 378-380.

Beiersdorfer, R.E., and Davis, W.E. 1994. "Suggestions for planning a class field trip." *Journal of College Science Teaching*, XXIII, 5, 307-311.

Bland, M., Saunders, G., and Frisch, J.K. 2007. "In defense of the lecture." *Journal of College Science Teaching*, XXXVII, 2, 10-13.

Bligh, D.A. 1971. *What's the Use of Lectures?* Exeter, Devon: D.A., and B. Bligh.

Bligh, D.A. 1972. *What's the Use of Lectures?* Harmondsworth, UK: Penguin.

Bligh, D. A. 2000. *What's the Use of Lectures?* San Francisco: Jossey-Bass.

Bloom, B.S., Engelhart, M.D., Furst, E.J., Hill, W.M., and Krathwohl, D.R. 1956. *Taxonomy of Educational Objectives, Handbook 1: Cognitive Domain.* New York: McKay.

Boehm, P. 2009. "Promoting Academic Integrity in Higher Education." Schoolcraft College.

Bork, A., Justice M., Weeks, S. 1981. *Learning with Computers.* Bedford, MA: Digital Press.

References

Brownstein, E., and Klein, R. 2006. "Blogs — applications in science education." *Journal of College Science Teaching*, XXXV, 6:18-22.

Burnstad, H. 2005. "Developing the environment for learning." In Greive D, (ed.). *Handbook II-Advanced Teaching Strategies for Adjunct and Part-time Faculty.* Ann Arbor, MI: Part-Time Press.

Cann, A., Badge, J., Johnson, S., and Moseley, A. 2009. "Twittering the students experience." Association for Learning Technology Online Newsletter, Issue 17, Monday, 19 October, 2009.

Cannon, R.E. 1990. "Experiments with writing to teach Microbiology." *The American Biology Teacher*, 52(3) 156-158.

Caprio, M.W. 1993. "Cooperative learning – the jewel among motivational teaching techniques." *Journal of College Science Teaching*, 5, 279-281.

Carter, J.L. 1993. "A national priority: providing quality field experiences for all students." *The American Biology Teacher*, 55(3), 140-143.

Carter, J.L., Hepper, F., Saigo, R.H., Twitty, G., and Walker, D. 1990. "The state of the Biology major." *Bioscience*, 40(9), 678-683.

Cheronis, N.D 1962. "The philosophy of laboratory instruction." *Journal of Chemical Education*, 39(2), 102-106.

Chickering, A.W., and Gamson, Z. 1987. "Seven principles for good practice in undergraduate education." American Association for Higher Education *Bulletin*, 39(7), 3-7.

Chizmar, J.F., and Ostrosky, A.L. 1998. "The one-minute paper: some empirical findings." *Journal of Economic Education*, 29(1), 3-10.

Cliburn, J.W. 1990. "Concept maps to promote meaningful learning." *Journal of College Science Teaching*, 4, 212-217.

Collins, Michael, A. 1979. "Helping students do better on tests." *The American Biology Teacher*, 41(4), 239-240.

Collins, Michael, A. 2004. "Using short pieces of writing (microthemes) to improve student learning." In Druger, M., Siebert, E.S., and Crow, L.W. (Eds.). *Teaching Tips – Innovations in Undergraduate Science Education,* 7-8. Arlington, VA: NSTA Press.

Collins, Michael, A., and Fletcher, P. 1985. "Using computer tests to identify areas for remedial teaching of Biology." *Journal of Computers in Mathematics and Science Teaching*, IV, 4, 36-37.

Cooper, J.L., and Robinson, P. 2000. "The argument for making large classes seem small." *New Directions for Teaching and Learning*. 81, 63-76.

De Graaf, G. 1984. "A parade with a difference." *Custos*, 13(9), 20-21.

Doran, R.L. 1972. "Misconceptions of selected science concepts held by elementary school students." *Journal of Research in Science Teaching*, 9(2), 127-137.

Dougherty, R.C., Bowen, C.W., Berger, T., and Rees, W. 1995. "Cooperative learning and enhanced communication." *Journal of Chemical Education*, 72, 9, 793-798.

Dubetz, T.A., Barreto, J.C., Deiros, D., Kakareka, J., Brown, D.W., and Ewald, C. 2008. "Multiple pedagogical reforms implemented in a university Science class to address diverse learning styles." *Journal of College Science Teaching*, XXXVIII, 2, 39-43.

Duncan, D. 2005. *Clickers in the Classroom: How to Enhance Science Teaching Using Classroom Response Systems.* San Francisco: Pearson Education/Addison-Wesley/Benjamin Cummings.

Eisner, S. 2004. "Teaching generation Y college students: three initiatives." *Journal of College Teaching and Learning*, 1(9) , 69-84.

Erickson, B.L., and Strommer, D.W. 1991. *Teaching College Freshmen.* San Francisco: Jossey-Bass.

Eves, R.L., and Davis, L.E. 2007. "Death by PowerPoint?" *Journal of College Science Teaching*, XXXVII, 5,8-9.

Ewing, M.S., Campbell, N.J., and Brown, M.J.M. 1987. "Improving student attitudes toward Biology by encouraging scientific literacy!" *The American Biology Teacher*, 49, 6, 348-350.

Felder, R.M. 1988. "How students learn: adapting teaching styles to learning styles." Proceedings, Frontiers in Education Conference, p. 289. Santa Barbara, CA: ASEE/IEEE.

Felder, R.M. 1993. "Reaching the second tier – learning and teaching styles in college science education." *Journal of College Science Teaching*, XXII, 5, 286-290.

References

Felder, R.M., and Silverman, L. 1988. "Learning and teaching styles in Engineering education." *Engineering Education*, 78, 7, 674-681.

Fisher, K.M., Lipson, J.I., Hildebrand, A.C., Miguel, L., Schoenberg, N., and Porter, N. 1986. "Student misconceptions and teacher assumptions in college Biology." *Journal of College Science Teaching* XV, 4, 276-280.

Foos, M. 1987. "Abstracts can enhance writing skills." *Journal of College Science Teaching*, XVI, 4, 254-255.

Gardner, H. 1991. *The Unschooled Mind: How Children Think and How Schools Should Teach.* New York: Basic Books.

Garner, R. 2006. "Humor in pedagogy: how ha-ha can lead to aha!" *College Teaching*, 54(1) 177-180.

Geske, J. 1992. "Overcoming the drawback of the large lecture class." *College Teaching*, 40(4) 151-154.

Gibbs, G., Habeshaw, S., and Habeshaw, T. 1992. *53 Interesting Things to do in Your Lectures.* Bristol, UK: Technical and Educational Services.

Godleski, E. 1984. "Learning style compatibility of Engineering students and faculty." Proceedings, Annual Frontiers in Education Conference. p. 362. Philadelphia ASEE/IEE.

Gray, T. & Madson, L. 2007. "Ten easy ways to engage your students." *College Teaching*, 55(2), 83-87.

Griffiths, D. 1973. Unpublished Ed.D. dissertation, Rutgers University, New Brunswick, NJ.

Guthrie, R.W., and Carlin, A. 2004. "Waking the dead: using interactive technology to engage passive listeners in the classroom." Proceedings of the Tenth Americas Conference on Information Systems, New York.

Hartley, J., and Davies, I.K. 1978. "Note-taking: a critical review." *Programmed Learning and Educational Technology*, 15, 3, 207-224.

Hartman, I.S. 1995. "Interactive and cooperative methods as an extension to examinations." *Journal of College Science Teaching*, XXIV, 6, 401-403.

Heppner, F. 2009. *Teaching the Large College Class: A Guidebook for Instructors with Multitudes.* San Francisco: Jossey-Bass.

Herreid, C.F. 2003. "The death of Problem-Based Learning?" *Journal of College Science Teaching*, 6, 364-366.

Herreid, C.F. 2006. "Clicker" cases: introducing case study teaching into large classrooms." *Journal of College Science Teaching*, XXXVI, 2,43-47.

Hofstein, A., and Lunetta, V.A. 1982. "The role of the laboratory in science teaching." *Review of Educational Research*, 52, 2, 201-217.

Horton, P.B., McConney, A.A., Gallo, M., Woods, A.L., Senn, G.J., and Hamelin, D. 1993. "An investigation of the effectiveness of Concept Mapping as an instructional tool." *Science Education*, 77(1), 95-111.

Hotchkiss, S.K., and Nellis, M.K. 1988. "Writing across the curriculum." *Journal of College Science Teaching*, XVIII, 1, 45-47.

Howe, M. and Godfrey, J. 1977. "Student note-taking as an aid to learning!" Exeter, NH: Exeter University Teaching Services.

Jacobson, T.E., and Wilson, L.D. 1991. "A bibliographic instruction program for college Biology students." *The American Biology Teacher*, 53(5), 298-300.

Johnstone, A.H., and Mahmoud, N.A. 1980. "Isolating topics of high perceive difficulty in school Biology." *Journal of Biological Education*, 14(2), 163-166.

Johnstone, A.M., and Percival, F. 1976. "Attention breaks in lectures." *Education in Chemistry*, 13, 2, 49-50.

Jungwirth, E. 1992. "The plan-a-test grid as a teaching and feedback instrument in Biology teacher education." *Journal of Biological Education*, 26, 1, 41-44.

Knowles, M. 1990. *The Adult Learner-A Neglected Species.* Houston, TX: Gulf Publishing.

Kolodiy, G. 1974. "Piagetian theory and college science teaching." *Journal of College Science Teaching*, III, 4, 261-262.

Kozma, R.B., Belle, L.W., and Williams, G.W. 1978. *Instructional Techniques in Higher Education.* Englewood Cliffs, NJ: Educational Technology Publications.

Larson, J.M. 1982. "Two cultures"– topics for general studies courses." *Journal of College Science Teaching*, XII, 2, 89-91.

References

Lawson, A.E. 1988. "A better way to teach Biology." *The American Biology Teacher*, 50(5), 266-273.

Leahy, R. 1994. "Microthemes: an experiment with very short writings." *College Teaching*, 42, 1, 15-18.

Leonard, W.H. 1988. "What research says about Biology laboratory instruction!" *The American Biology Teacher*, 50(5), 303-306.

Lewis, K.G. 1994. *Teaching large classes (How to do it well and remain sane).* In Prichard, K.W., and Sawyer, R.M. (eds.). *Handbook of College Teaching: Theory and Application*, p. 319-343. London: Greenwood Press.

Lipson, A. and Tobias, S. 1991. "Some of our best – Why do college students leave science?" *Journal of College Science Teaching*, XX, 92-95.

Lloyd, D.H. 1968. "A concept of improvement of learning response in the taught lesson." *Visual Education*, October, 23-25.

Lord, T. 2008. "We know how to improve science understanding in students, so why aren't college professors embracing it?" *Journal of College Science Teaching*, XXXVIII, 1, 66-70.

MacGregor, J., Cooper, J. L., Smith, K. A., & Robinson, P. 2000. Editor's notes. *Strategies for Energizing Large Classes: From Small Groups to Learning Communities.* New Directions for Teaching and Learning, no. 81., San Francisco: Jossey-Bass.

Mager, R.F. 1984. *Preparing Instructional Objectives.* Belmont, California: Lake Management and Training.

Martin, L.V. 1985. "Exam self-analysis – helping students accept responsibility." *Journal of College Science Teaching*, XIV, 5, 424-425.

McCarthy, B. 1987. *The 4-MAT Systems: Teaching to Learning Styles With Right-Left Mode Techniques*, Barrington, IL: Excel, Inc.

McCauley, M.M. 1977. "Personality variables: Modal profiles that characterize the various fields of science and what they mean for education?" *Journal of College Science Teaching*, VII, 114-120.

McKeachie, W.J. 2002. *McKeachie's Teaching Tips: Strategies, Research, and Theory for College and University Teachers.* Boston: Houghton-Mifflin.

McKeachie, W.J., and Svinicki, M. 2006. *McKeachie's Teaching Tips: Strategies, Research, and Theory for College and University Teachers.* 12th edition. Boston: Houghton-Mifflin.

McKinnon, J.W. 1971. "Earth Science, density and the college freshmen." *Journal of Geological Education*, 19, 218-220.

McLeish, J. 1968. *The Lecture Method. Cambridge Monographs on Teaching Methods.* Cambridge, U.K.: Cambridge Institute of Education.

Melear, C.T. 1990. "Cognitive processes in the Curry learning style framework as measured by the learning style profile and the Meyers-Briggs type indicator among non-majors in Biology." Dissertation Abstracts International, 51-1: 127A.

Miller, R.I. 1975. *Developing Programs for Faculty Evaluation.* San Francisco: Jossey-Bass.

Moore, R. 1994. "Writing to learn Biology." *Journal of College Science Teaching*, XXIII, 5, 289-295.

Nastase, A.J., and Scharmann, L.C. 1991. "Non-major's biology: enhanced curricular considerations." *The American Biology Teacher*, 53(1), 31-36.

National Education Association, 1975. <www.new.org/about-nea/code.html.>

National Task Force on Undergraduate Physics. 2002. Report on SPIN-UP (Strategic Programs for Innovation in Physics).

Novak, J.D. 1993. "How do we learn our lesson?" *The Science Teacher*, 7, (October), 50-55.

O'Banion, T. 1997. *"A Learning College for the 21st Century."* Phoenix, Arizona: Oryx Press.

Okebukola, P.A. 1990. "Attaining meaningful learning of concepts in Genetics and Ecology: an examination of the potency of the concept-mapping technique." *Journal of Research in Science Teaching*, 27(5), 493-504.

Orien, N., and Hofstein, M. 1991. "The measurement of students' attitudes towards scientific field trips." *Science Education*, 75(5), 513-523.

Orzechowski, R.F. 1995. "Factors to consider before introducing active learning into a large, lecture-based course." *Journal of College Science Teaching*, XXIV, 5, 347-349.

References

Randall, M. 2000. "A guide to good teaching: be slow and inefficient." *The Chronicle of Higher Education*, December 8, B24.

Rowe, M.B. 1982. "Getting Chemistry off the killer course list." *Journal of Chemical Education*, 60(11), 954-956.

Ruhl, K.L., Hughes, C.A., and Schloss, P.J. 2007. "Using the Pause Procedure to enhance lecture recall." *Teacher Education and Special Education*, 10(1),14-18.

Russell, H.R. 1990. *Ten-Minute Field Trips: A Teacher's Guide to Using the School Grounds for Environmental Science!* Second Edition. Washington, D.C.: National Science Teachers Association.

Russell, I.J., Hendricson, W.D., and Hervert, R.J. 1984. "Effects of lecture information density on medical student achievement." *Journal of Medical Education*, 59(11), 881-889.

Salomon, J. 1994. "The diverse classroom." In Frye, B. (ed). *Teaching in College-A Resource for College Teachers*. Elyria OH: Info-Tec.

Samples, B. 1994. "Instructional Diversity – teaching to your students' strengths." *The Science Teacher*, 61(3), 14-17.

Schwab, Joseph and Brandwein, Paul. 1962. *The Teaching of Science. Two Essays.* Cambridge, MA: Harvard University Press.

Shuell, T.J. 1987. "Cognitive Psychology and conceptual change." *Science Education*, 71(2), 239-250.

Shulman, L.D., and Tamir, P. 1973. "Research on teaching in the Natural Sciences." In Travers, R.M.V. (Ed.). *Second Handbook on Research in Teaching.* Chicago: Rand-McNally.

Steed, M. 1992. "Stella, a simulation construction kit: cognitive process and educational implications." *Journal of Computers in Mathematics and Science Teaching*, II, I, 39-52.

Sundberg, M.D., and Armstrong, J.E. 1993. "The status of laboratory instruction for introductory Biology in U.S. universities." *The American Biology Teacher*, 55(3), 144-146.

Tamir, P., and Lunetta, V.N. 1981. "Inquiry-related tasks in high-school Science textbooks." *Science Education*, 65, 477-484.

Tharp, G.D. 1993. "The connection between personality type and achievement in college Biology." *Journal of College Science Teaching*, XXII, 5, 276-278.

Tobias, S. 1989. "Writing to learn Science and Mathematics." In Connolly, P.H., and Vilardi, T. (Eds.). *Writing to Learn Science and Mathematics.* New York: Teachers College Press.

Tobias, S. 1990. *"They're Not Dumb. They're Different – Stalking the Second Tier."* Tucson, Arizona: Research Corporation.

Trombulak, S., and Sheldon, S. 1989. "The real value of writing to learn in Biology." *Journal of College Science Teaching*, XVIII, 6, 384-386.

Tufte, E.R. 2006. *The Cognitive Style of PowerPoint: Pitching out Corrupts Within.* Cheshire, CT: Graphic Press.

Van Rooyen, H.G. 1994. "The quest for optimum clarity of presentation: context creation as teaching skill." *The American Biology Teacher*, 56(3), 146-150.

Wandersee, J.H. 1985. "Can the history of science help science educators anticipate students' misconceptions?" *Journal of Research in Science Teaching*, 23(7), 581-597.

Watson, S.B. 1992. "The essential elements of cooperative learning." *The American Biology Teacher*, 54, 2, 84-86.

Watson, S.B., and Marshall, J.E. 1995. "Effects of cooperative incentives and heterogeneous arrangement on achievement and interaction of cooperative learning groups in a college Life Science course." *Journal of Research in Science Teaching*, 32(3), 291-299.

Weaver, R.L., and Cotrell, H.W. 1987. "Lecturing: essential communication strategies." In Weimer, M.G. (Ed.). *Teaching Large Classes Well. New Directions for Teaching and Learning*, no. 32, 57-69. San Francisco: Jossey-Bass.

Weimer, M. 2002. *Improving College Teaching.* San Francisco: Jossey-Bass.

Wesley, Walter G. and Wesley, Beverly A., 1990. "Concept mapping: a brief introduction," *The Teaching Professor,* October.

Wilson, J.T. and Stensvold, M.S. 1991. "Improving laboratory instruction: an interpretation of research." *Journal of College Science Teaching*, XX, 6, 350-353.

Work, J.C. 1979. "Reducing three papers to ten: a method for literature courses." In Stanford, G. (Ed.). *How to Handle the Paper Load. Classroom Practices in Teaching English.* p. 80-88. Urbana, Illinois: NCTE, 1979-80.

Wright, E.L. 1981. "Fifteen simple discrepant events that teach science principles and concepts." *School Science and Mathematics*, 81, 575-580.

Wright, E.L. and Govindarajan, G. 1992. "Stirring the Biology teaching pot with discrepant events." *The American Biology Teacher*, 54(4), 205-211.

Wright, E.L. and Govindarajan, G. 1995. *Teaching with Scientific Conceptual Discrepancies: Unlocking the Mind to Problem-Solving Using Simple Discrepant Events that Illustrate Science Concepts and Principles.* Manhattan, Kansas: Kansas State University.

Wulff, D. H., Nyquist, J. D., & Abbott, R. D. 1987. "Students' perceptions of large classes." In K. E. Eble (Series Ed.) & M. G. Weimer (Vol. Ed.), *New Directions for Teaching and Learning*: Vol. 32. *Teaching Large Classes Well.* San Francisco: Jossey-Bass.

Yazedjian, A., and Kolkhorst, B.B. 2007. "Implementing small-group activities in large classes." *College Teaching*, 55(4), 164-169.

Index

A

B

Index

C

Campbell, N.J. 95
Cann, A. 69
Cannon, R.E. 137, 138
Caprio, M.W. 106, 107
Carlin, A. 72
Carter, J.L. 145, 146
case studies 112. *See also* alternative instructional strategies
Center for Academic Integrity 33
cheating. *See* academic dishonesty
Chickering, A.W. 9, 115
Chizmar, J.F. 119
classroom assessment 19, 36
Cliburn, J.W. 111
clickers 71, 80. *See* student response systems
Code of Ethics of the Education Profession 31
cognitive domain 45
cognitive learning 45
collaborative learning 25, 41, 46
Collins, Michael A. 1, 128, 137
community-centered learning 17
Company Magazine 38
computers 6, 142, 158
computers and laboratories. *See* laboratory sessions
concept maps 109. *See also* alternative instructional strategies
context creation 113. *See also* alternative instructional strategies
cooperative learning 38, 40, 106, 108. *See also* alternative instructional
    strategies
Cooper, J.L. 74, 78
Cottrell, H.W. 78
course content 23, 43, 49, 50, 67, 117, 122, 125, 134, 137
course description 29
course objectives 20, 34, 45, 49, 121, 123, 124
course outline 34, 55, 56, 60
course requirements 49
critical thinking 25, 40, 141

D

Davies, I.K. 100, 116
Davis, L.E. 65, 66
Davis, W.E. 146
De Graaf, G. 113
Desire2Learn 57, 69
diversity 43, 44

H

handouts 20, 34, 77
Hartley, J. 100, 116
Hartman, I.S. 126, 127
Harvard University 112
Heppner, F. 82
Herreid, C.F. 71, 72, 73, 108, 112
Hofstein, M. 146
Horton, P.B. 111
Hotchkiss, S.K. 132
humor 24, 27

I

icebreaker 23, 53
instructional objectives 15
Internet 28, 37, 38, 64, 65, 66, 68, 76

J

Jacobson, T.E. 133
Jungwirth, E. 124
Justice, Madeline 33
Johnstone, A.H. 152
Journal of College Science Teaching 155

K

Kidd, J. 70, 71
Klein, R. 68
Knowles, Malcolm 39
Kolkhorst, B.B. 77
Kolodiy, G. 92
Kozma, R.B. 115, 116

L

laboratory sessions 140, 142, 144
laissez-faire classroom 49
Larson, J.M. 94
Lay, Bob 37
Lawson, A.E. 104
Leahy, R. 136
learning college 17
learning management systems 69
learning styles 10, 12, 87, 88, 89, 90, 93, 97, 154

M

N

Index

O

O'Banion, Terry 85
office hours 30, 52, 56, 60, 71, 77, 82
Okebukola, P.A. 110
open-ended questions 25
Orien, N. 146
Orzechowski, R.F. 127
Ostrosky, A.L. 119

P

pedagogy 38, 74, 86
Piaget's Theory of Intellectual Development 91
plagiarism 32, 55, 57, 59. *See also* academic dishonesty
planning for teaching 52
PLB. *See* problem-based learning
portfolio 46, 96, 139
PowerPoint 8, 52, 65, 67, 70, 75, 76, 79, 97, 117
presentation software 65, 66, 76, 117
problem-based learning 108. *See also* alternative instructional strategies
projects 49, 50, 81, 139
psychomotor domain 45

R

Ramapo State University 37
Randall, M. 117
reinforcement 19, 26, 49, 120
role playing 38
Rowe, M.B. 97
Ruhl, K.L. 100
Russell, I.J. 117

S

Salomon, J. 44
Samples, B. 87
Scharmann, L.C. 94
Schwab, J. 146
scientific method 61, 141
Second Life 65, 70, 71
Sheldon, S. 137, 138
Shuell, T.J. 9, 10
Silverman, L. 88
simulations. *See* laboratory sessions
Spandel, V. 139

W

X

Y

If you found this book helpful, you'll want to check out these other titles:

Handbook II: Advanced Strategies for Adjunct and Part-time Faculty by Donald Greive

Handbook II: Advanced Teaching Strategies carries on the tradition of practical and readable instructional guides that began with *A Handbook for Adjunct & Part-time Faculty* (now in its 7th edition!)

Intended for adjuncts who have already mastered the basics and for the managers of adjunct faculty, *Handbook II: Advanced Teaching Strategies* offers in-depth coverage of some of the topics you just read about like andragogy, collaborative learning, syllabus construction, and testing. But this manual also goes beyond these topics to discuss specific teaching techniques for critical thinking, problem solving, large class instruction and distance learning assignments.

Handbook II: Advanced Teaching Strategies gives you expert and current strategies to take your teaching to the next level. Available in paperback for $19.00 each.

A Handbook for Adjunct/Part-Time Faculty & Teachers of Adults, Seventh Edition by Donald Greive

This is more than just a teacher's manual! This little powerhouse helps adjuncts tackle the day-to-day problems associated with teaching part-time. From course planning to teaching adult students, this book offers practical suggestions, strategies and advice. With over 180,000 copies sold, *A Handbook* provides adjuncts with the contents of a first-rate teaching workshop for a fraction of the price. Available in paperback for $18.00 each.

NOTE: *A Handbook* & *Handbook II* are available in a set for $35 per set.

FAQ's...

How can I place an orders?

Orders can be placed **by mail** to Part-Time Press, P.O. Box 130117, Ann Arbor, MI 48113-0117, **by phone** at **(**734)930-6854, **by fax** at (734)665-9001, and **via the Internet** at http://www. Part-TimePress.com.

How much do I pay if I want multiple copies?

Each Part-Time Press book has a quantity discount schedule available. The schedule for *Teaching in the Sciences* is:

1-9 copies--$25 each   **10-49 copies**--$23 each
50-99 copies--$20 each   **100 or more copies**--$18 each

How can I pay for orders?

Orders can be placed on **a purchase order** or can be paid by **check** or **credit card** (Visa/Mastercard, Discover or AMEX.)

How will my order be shipped?

Standard shipping to a continental U.S. street address is via **UPS-Ground Service**. Foreign shipments or U.S. post office box addresses go through the **U.S. Postal Service** and express shipments via **UPS-2nd Day**, or **UPS-Next Day**. Shipping and handling charges are based on the dollar amount of the shipment, and a fee schedule is shown on the next page.

What if I'm a reseller like a bookstore or wholesaler?

Resellers get a standard **20 percent discount** off of the single copy retail price, or may choose to receive the multiple copy discount.

Teaching in the Sciences: A Handbook

Part-Time Press Books: Order Form

Qty	Title	Unit $$	Total
	Teaching in the Sciences	**$25.00**	
	Getting Down to Business	**$25.00**	
	Going the Distance: A Handbook for Part-Time & Adjunct Faculty Who Teach Online, Rev. 1st ed.	**$15.00**	
	Handbook for Adjunct/Part-Time Faculty, 7th ed.	**$18.00**	
	Handbook II: Advanced Teaching Strategies	**$19.00**	
	Managing Adjunct/Part-Time Faculty	**$30.00**	
	Teaching Strategies and Techniques, 5th ed.	**$12.00**	
	Teaching & Learning in College	**$25.00**	
		Subtotal	
		Shipping	
		Total	

Purchaser/Payment Information

☐   *Check (payable to The Part-Time Press)*

☐   *Credit Card # ———————————————— Exp. ————*

   CVV# ————

☐   *Purchase Order # ————————————————*

Name ————————————————————————

Institution ————————————————————————

Address ———————————— City/ST/Zip ————————

Ph:———————————— E-mail: ————————————

Shipping Schedule:

1-4 books $6.00

5+ books   8 percent of the purchase price

Part-Time Press: P.O. Box 130117, Ann Arbor, MI 48113-0117
Ph: 734-930-6854   Fax: 734-665-9001   Email: orders@part-timepress.com
Order securely online: http://www.Part-TimePress.com